Evening at Symphony

Evening at Symphony

A Portrait of the
Boston Symphony Orchestra

Janet Baker-Carr

Illustrated with Photographs

Houghton Mifflin Company Boston 1977

The author is grateful to the following for permission to reprint
from copyrighted sources:
The Atlantic Monthly Press for extracts from *Life and Letters of Henry Lee
Higginson* by Bliss Perry. Copyright 1921 by Bliss Perry.
W. Heffer & Sons Ltd., Cambridge, England, for extracts from *The
Orchestra, From Beethoven to Berlioz* by Adam Carse. Copyright 1948
by W. Heffer & Sons Ltd.
Alfred A. Knopf, Inc., for extracts from *Memoirs of Hector Berlioz:
From 1803–1865*, translated by David Cairns. Copyright © 1969
by David Cairns.
Mary Manning Howe for extracts from *The Boston Symphony Orchestra*
by M. A. DeWolfe Howe, published by Houghton Mifflin Company, 1931.
Copyright © 1977 by Janet Baker-Carr and WGBH Educational Foundation, Inc.

Library of Congress Cataloging in Publication Data
Baker-Carr, Janet.
Evening at Symphony.

1. Boston Symphony Orchestra.   2.   Musicians — Massa-
chusetts — Boston.   I. Title.
ML200.8.B72S94   1977   785'.06'274461   77-9305
ISBN 0-395-25697-6

Printed in the United States of America

A 10 9 8 7 6 5 4 3 2 1

"When sounds stir within me, I always hear
the full orchestra; I know what to expect
of instrumentalists, who are capable
of almost everything."

BEETHOVEN

Acknowledgments

Evening at Symphony is about people who have contributed to the finest traditions of composition and performance of orchestral music. I am grateful to them all. I am particularly grateful to the Boston Symphony Orchestra, which was enthusiastic and helpful in the book's preparation. I am grateful to WGBH — Channel 2, which sponsors "Evening at Symphony." Without the station's support, this book could not have been written. I am grateful to Harvard's Institute in Arts Administration for giving me a leave of absence to work on the book and to the Harvard Music Library for aid in the research. I thank the colleague who suggested that I write the book and my editor at Houghton Mifflin whose generous support and advice made the writing a pleasure.

JANET BAKER-CARR

Contents

Illustrations

*All photographs in the book, unless otherwise credited, were obtained
courtesy of the Boston Symphony Orchestra or WGBH, Boston.*

Evening at Symphony

Major Henry Lee Higginson, founder and sustainer of the Boston Symphony Orchestra, photograph of a portrait by John Singer Sargent.

Chapter One

Major Henry Lee Higginson, Founder of the BSO

"Ever since my boyhood I have longed to have a part in some good work which could leave a lasting mark on the world. Today we have a noble orchestra — the work of our hands which gives joy and comfort to many."
— Major Higginson

IT WAS IN THE 1850s, while he was a music student in Vienna, that Henry Lee Higginson had the idea of and started to form the plan for the Boston Symphony Orchestra. That dream was to take nearly thirty years to come true. Today, nearly one hundred years after its first concert, the orchestra remains remarkably close to its original plan.

The Boston Symphony Orchestra was one of America's first permanent resident symphony orchestras. Founded in the interest of good music and for the benefit of his fellow citizens, Major Higginson's orchestra became the standard by which others were judged, a source of civic achievement and of national pride. Unlike other great public benefactors of his day, Major Higginson did not have vast fortunes at his disposal. Rather, he founded the orchestra with money he had recently earned and committed himself to support it with money to be earned in the future. In this way he sustained the orchestra for nearly forty years.

Until his death in 1919, Henry L. Higginson held a conspicuous place in the public life of his country. By virtue of a large, active correspondence, he was the friend of congressmen, cabinet members, and presidents — and, when he felt it proper, their critic. A personal letter from President Wilson, dated December 10, 1914, begins: "Your letters always stimulate me . . ."

Deeply committed to education, he was instrumental in the founding of Radcliffe College; he was also a generous benefactor of Harvard University and one of its Overseers.

He was a Puritan both by birth and by preference, a man who believed in the virtue of hard work. He was shrewd and hard-headed, but he thought of institutions and problems in terms of people, and "the number of folks who are to be smoothed, admonished, touched up, is wonderful." His assessment of people was not always accurate. Several times he came perilously close to bankruptcy, but his whimsical sense of humor never left him. As he once recalled:

> Truth telling is essential in business but socially it is very diverting to lie. For instance, I was standing on the corner of Park and Tremont Streets the other day when a motor came down the hill, locked wheels with another, and turned over. In a moment a crowd was buzzing round; it was just like kicking a hornet's nest. A lady came by — uncertain of age — nondescript clothes, flat heels, carrying a bag — you know the type, you see them in Boston. Addressing no particular person, she said as she passed me, "Anybody hurt? Anybody hurt?"
>
> Very politely I replied with a bow, "I hope so, madame."
>
> She looked at me sharply, and discovering that I was old and gray and probably deaf, she repeated the inquiry in a louder tone. "Yes, madame, I heard the first time: I said, 'I hope so'; think how disappointed all the people would be if nobody were hurt."
>
> Murmuring, "What a wretched, wicked old man!" she walked about ten feet, then turning, she came back, and scrutinizing me closely, said, "Aren't you Mr. Higginson?'
>
> "No, Madame."
>
> "You look very much like him."
>
> "I have been told so." I lifted my hat and bowed most politely as the lady walked away in a quandary.

Henry L. Higginson, proud public citizen, was a man of relentless courage. At the end, when he was old and frail and had survived several operations, it became necessary for him to have yet another. He refused to take the elevator down to the street, where the car waited to take him to the hospital. Instead, with his head held high, he slowly walked down the four flights. He died that night.

Henry Lee Higginson's ancestors came from England to Salem, Massachusetts, in 1629. The family has remained in New England providing it with civic leaders, ministers, and merchants noted for their piety, patriotism, and benevolence. Although there was one minister who was reputed to have a beautiful singing voice, there is no indication of an abiding family interest in music or its performance.

George Higginson, Henry's father, married Mary Cabot Lee and they moved to New York. His mercantile venture failed in the panic of 1837 and they returned to Boston, bringing with them the young Henry, aged four.

Their life was simple and embedded in the New England tradition. Later in his life Henry looked back and wrote:

> We lived in the narrowest way, and got on very well . . . [I] had a pleasant boyhood. Everything was done in a very small way, and my father and mother both worked pretty hard. My father was one of thirteen children, was put to work at the age of twelve in an office and stayed in business until 1874, when he was seventy years old. He was a kindly, industrious, sensible man, with a remarkable "nose" for character . . . when he was earning very little money, he passed much of his time and any spare pennies possible in charitable work.

His mother, who died of tuberculosis when he was fourteen,

> was unusually intelligent and attractive, as I now know from the various older men and younger men who used to come to our house and dine. We had meat — chiefly corned beef — about five times a week at dinner, had no butter, never saw an egg, had plenty of potatoes, and baked apples, and milk.

Historically, the family took great pride in their patriotism:

> We all took some interest in public affairs, and when the Revolution of 1848 came in Europe, it interested us much. I had a very strong feeling about our country, and was very proud of it, thought it had no faults, could not conceive of living under any other government, and was delighted with the revolutions in Europe.

The family also had strong abolitionist convictions. As young boys, Henry and his three brothers attended the meetings in Faneuil Hall that were concerned with slavery, and there they heard

Daniel Webster speak. Henry always felt he was a liberal and a reformer and that those feelings grew as he did.

The Higginson clan was closely knit and very large: Higginsons, Cabots, Lees, Lowells, Perkinses, and Morses all called each other cousin. Not all the Higginsons were wealthy. George Higginson worked in a counting house on India Wharf when his family was growing up and lived carefully. However, Henry L. Higginson followed the path of Boston's wealthy and privileged to the Latin School, which was free, and went on to Harvard in 1851. There were three hundred and four students in the college at the time. Daniel Webster and Edward Everett were among Harvard's Overseers; Longfellow was a professor. There were four courses open to freshmen: history, mathematics, Greek, and Latin. Chapel was required early each morning.

His eyes, which had previously given trouble, now were of grave concern, and by midyear Henry was forced to leave Harvard and take a cure in Vermont, which did not work. Early that spring he made arrangements to go on a walking tour through Germany and Switzerland. And so, on a Saturday afternoon in May of 1852, before his eighteenth birthday, Henry Lee Higginson sailed from New York to England on the packet *Constitution*.

Henry Lee Higginson maintained a voluminous and lively correspondence all his life. His theory about letter writing was simple: Just write the letter as if you were talking to the person. Then go back and cross out the adjectives and most of the adverbs and the letter will probably say what you wish. The letters to his father reveal a young man of profound depth, humor, and enthusiastic innocence.

Hardly had he got to London before he went to see every opera and concert possible. In his journal one night, soon after his arrival, he wrote: "Very impassioned acting. Splendid acting and orchestra. Everything beautiful, and splendid, and delicious. English ladies very much like ours, a little plumper." The future friend and critic of presidents, international banker, and man of affairs who addressed his letters to William James as "My dear Boy" recalled this experience on arriving in Ostend:

> A large fellow seized my luggage on his shoulders and marched me
> up to the hotel. There a very civil man with a large beard bowed to

me and addressed me in two tongues, and then said: "Do you want a room?" I said "I do." Having got that room, I was afraid to go downstairs to get anything to eat, because I had no words, and, therefore, I went to bed without supper.

After an energetic walking tour through Switzerland he traveled through Germany, listening to concerts and opera wherever he went. That winter he made an extended stay in Dresden in order to learn the language and to hear the music there. Wagner had been the conductor at the opera house until 1848, and his influence and work were still felt and celebrated. In addition to symphony concerts there were more intimate concerts in the coffee houses, where one could eat ice cream or drink coffee and listen to the music for just a few pennies.

Life was simple and happy. He wrote: "My digestion was that of a horse. Bread soup was common . . . we had all kinds of sausages . . . of course there were no habits of washing, and when I asked for a bathtub, I had to buy one." He heard Wagner's *Tannhäuser*, oratorios by Handel, and French, German, and Italian operas. He also rented a piano so that he could practice and went to galleries and museums. From Dresden he went to Prague and on to Vienna, where a highlight was "the rehearsal of the great concert in the theater. Mozart's Requiem and the Ninth Symphony of Beethoven with a chorus and singing. The finest concert I think I ever heard."

As the moment drew near for his return he tried to extend his stay, and he wrote to his father of a feeling that remained with him for life: "I do not believe there is anything more refining than music, no greater or stronger protector against evil, and at least for me it has done much."

He found it hard to leave Europe, where almost every town had opera and concerts, but after a trip to Paris and London he returned in September 1853 to Boston.

The following three years were difficult. His friends and classmates were entering their junior year at Harvard and Henry could not join them. Nor could he enter as a sophomore. Nor would he as a freshman. Instead, he chose to pursue his studies privately with Samuel Eliot in Louisburg Square on Beacon Hill; in the evenings there were pleasant hours for music-making with his Harvard classmates at the Lowells' house in Cambridge. This arrangement lasted for eighteen months. His father then insisted that he go to work and got him a job in the office of Messrs. Samuel and Edward Austin, India Merchants, on India Wharf. There he served for eighteen months as sole clerk and bookkeeper, keeping track of the monthly shipments coming from Calcutta, Manila, Java, or Australia. Henry must have done well, for when he left the business he received a fine recommendation to go to India in the employ of a friend who had a large and profitable business there. But he demurred.

While studying with Samuel Eliot he had become absorbed by Emerson's doctrine of individualism (later in life he kept a picture of Emerson over his desk). All his life Henry had a strong natural affection for other men. In his early twenties, one of his greatest pleasures was to sit up all night with Stephen Perkins, Charles Lowell, and James Savage in deep discussion. There was plenty of political ferment to discuss.

Henry and Charley Lowell were two of twenty thousand on June 2, 1854, who followed the last fugitive slave captured in Massachusetts from State Street down to Long Wharf. Under the Fugitive Slave Act, Anthony Burns, who had been working in a tailor's shop in Boston, was to be returned to serfdom. Angry and ashamed, Henry turned to his friend and said, "Charley, it will come to us to set this right." Charley, Stephen Perkins, and James Savage were all to die in the Civil War.

There were discussions and public meetings about support for Kansas to come into the Union as a free state; Henry and some of his friends thought about going out to Kansas to help. John Brown's fight against border ruffians at Osawatomie took place, and through tears he had said, "There will be no more peace in this land until slavery is done for."

At this time, fortunes in Boston were being made in ventures closely or directly related to slaves. An antislavery society was active in Boston; nevertheless Henry and his friends felt like angry radicals in a conservative community.

The ferment Henry was feeling was not just political; it was also the private turmoil of a young man who had yet to find a way to be his own person. He was restless in a job he did not find completely absorbing. So when Charley Lowell wrote to him from Italy, ill and lonely, in November 1856, Henry, Stephen Perkins, and Jim Savage went immediately to be with and help their friend.

The next months were happy and carefree. Charley, who was better, and his three friends traveled about Europe, making excursions up into the mountains and visiting friends. By spring many people they knew were in Europe and they met in Rome for the Easter festivities. Four days were spent walking in the hills of Rome. Stephen, Charley, and Henry formed the plan that they would buy two horses and a two-wheeled gig and over the summer months drive north from Rome to Florence and Venice and up through Bohemia to Dresden. This they did:

> We start from five to six (sometimes later) and drive 'til it gets warm, stop several hours, feed our horses and eat, read, and sleep 'til it is cool, when we drive on. We average thirty to thirty-five miles a day; the horses are good for fifty any day.

On June 23 they reached Venice, where Henry, sitting in Saint Mark's Square at dawn, wrote to his father that he thought Venice to be the most charming city in the world, and Saint Mark's Square unrivaled in beauty. Although Henry and his two friends were delighted with their adventure and their mode of traveling, he did note in his letter: "One great charm of Venice is that you never see a horse there. One takes a gondola for a long distance!"

They pushed on, heading for the Tyrolean Alps:

> All day long we drove nearer to them, and at night slept at their bases. A strange feeling of excitement seizes one on getting among mountains. One not only finds delight in their beauty, their wondrous lights and shadows chasing one another along their sides, up and down their valleys, their gushing, dashing streams, their beautiful clothing of trees and turf, or, high up, of grey rock and snow, while down below their bases are covered with pastures and cultivated fields of grain, with here and there a cluster of cottages. In all this one delights, and really loves them too. But beyond it all is a wonderful exhilaration amounting to excitement about them. Else whence comes the intense, overwhelming passion to go over high passes and mountains?

The little band of travelers arrived in Salzburg on July 18 and continued on, down the Danube from Linz to Vienna, where Henry wrote:

I often wish you were here, old Daddy to drive about with me in the cart; it would jolt your bones a bit, but you would soon be used to it, and only feel hungry, not sore, at the end of the day. You would enjoy very much the scenery, which is daily before us. This way of travelling is very good and cheap, reckoned day by day.

Once again they turned north, passing through Bohemia to Prague, reaching Dresden on August 31. Their adventure had taken them more than three months — Charley was much stronger and more cheerful.

Henry finally realized the plan he had been brooding over: to stay in Europe and study music seriously. He wrote: "As everyone has some particular object of supreme interest to himself, so I have music. It is almost my inner world; without it, I miss much, with it I am happier and better . . . the pleasure of playing, and still more of singing myself, is indescribable." He was not sure what would come of his studies, "But this is clear, I have then improved my own powers, which is every man's duty. I have a resource to which I can always turn with delight, however the world may go with me. I am studying for my own good and pleasure." He also felt that he was carrying out one of his father's wishes, that of "making an unperishable capital in education. My money may fly away, my knowledge cannot. One belongs to the world, the other to me."

Henry chose to be in Vienna so that he might combine the study of theory, instrumental music, and singing to best advantage. He found Vienna to be a most pleasant city, with the best opera in the world. He arranged for simple, inexpensive lodgings and found a restaurant where "I am sure to get bona-fide articles and no grease."

Fortunately, he had recently received a legacy from a grandfather and an uncle and, while the sum was small, it insured that he could be financially independent.

Although the study of music took up much of his time, he did speculate on the market profitably in indigo, jute, and other products from East India. He asked his father to keep him in touch with the market at home. He also followed the market in London and maintained his strong interest in American and European politics and the current wars in India and China.

In the diaries of Henry's first trip to Europe, almost every entry had contained some excited reference to a performance of music and the detailed description of his own response to it. It was as if music had entered his life at that point with a loud fanfare, and in his own delight and exuberance he needed to hear and see as many performances as possible.

On this second trip Henry was devoted to his study of music. He had nine lessons a week in voice, piano, and composition; attended two lectures a week on theory; and spent four or five hours a night practicing. His enjoyment of the music he studied and of the performances he heard became intense but far more private.

His letters and journals at that time were concerned with the troublesome state of the world and family matters. At twenty-two he was already a philosopher. In answer to a letter from his father, who worried about the progress of the younger sons at school, he wrote this remarkable reply:

> Just remember, father, men are differently made, and because a boy will not study at school or win honors at college, he is not necessarily going to the devil, and his father does not need to wear "a thorn in his heart," or feel "deep mental anguish." Take the boys as they are, mend them if you can, and at all events don't worry. You only chafe yourself and them to the bone. 'T is not the way to cause happiness to anyone, yourself or them. I should think that you would, in the course of your life, have found pride of any kind a most wearing, burdensome article. Do not be proud in any way; take and give; it is the usual fault of good people. There is a theory that a "proper" kind of pride is a good thing; there never was such nonsense — vanity is better. Just think once again in a quiet half-hour, and you will see it. Do not be proud or ashamed of your children; you're not responsible for them. They are beings who stand on their own legs, and have volition just like you. If they won't do what you wish, don't worry about it. I dislike exceedingly to see you day by day wearing yourself by worrying because the children are not angels. Be at peace, father, make lots of money, and enjoy the remainder of your days on this ball. If you cannot beg pleasure one way, get it another.

Henry lived as he was accustomed to, frugally, and he gave lessons to help defray his expenses, which were not always his own.

He lived by what he once wrote to his father: "What is money good for, if not to spend for one's friends and to help them?" There was a time in Vienna when he contemplated buying an Austrian brewery and, later, starting a business that would import Hungarian wines to America.

The young man worked eight or ten hours a day on his music, and only a surgeon's ineptitude caused him to stop. In those days bloodletting was used to relieve headaches; Henry returned to practicing too soon after such a treatment and permanently disabled his arm for playing the piano over an extended time. He knew then that his hopes for a life as a musician would not be fulfilled, although he perhaps could teach. Within the year, and at his father's request and growing insistence, Henry left Vienna, visited friends in Paris and London, and returned to America.

The city in which he had lived and studied in the late 1850s was the Vienna of just a generation after Beethoven's death. It was caught up in the fanatical idealization of Beethoven's music. All across Europe, music was in some sense the symbol of recently won freedoms. Beethoven the revolutionary, Beethoven the progressive giant, inspired an idealism about human hopes and aspirations that brought performances of his and other music close to being a religious experience. The Viennese went to concerts for pleasure but even more for spiritual enlightenment. The institution of orchestral concerts that had evolved over the previous eighty years was now in one of its golden periods, especially in Vienna. The rich legacy Mozart had composed while living in Vienna was only sixty years old, Beethoven had been dead only thirty years, much of Schubert's music was less than twenty years old. Schumann, Mendelssohn, and Chopin had only recently died, and Clara Schumann, Berlioz, and Liszt were very much alive. Tchaikovsky, César Franck, and Grieg were alive, as were Wagner, Verdi, and Rossini. Brahms had already written some of his great piano works; he was about to move to Vienna, and in a few years would compose his first symphony. Bruckner was the organist in Linz Cathedral and studied in Vienna.

An exceptionally high standard for music journalism was being set at the time. Music became the source of literary composition. Henry Higginson's friend A. W. Thayer was in Vienna, writing his

monumental *Life of Beethoven*. Word of new composers, new
works, and the rediscovery of old ones were topics of lively articles
and heated discussion. Music was the life's blood to a war-weary
Europe.

That a performance of music could also be an experience of spiritual enlightenment and pleasure to a strife-torn people was a concept that appealed greatly to Henry. He sat through many concerts
that he did not necessarily enjoy or the music of which was not to
his taste. He did it for his own enlightenment. "Education is the
object of man, and it seems to me the duty of us all to help in it,
each according to his means and in his sphere," he wrote. Henry's
sphere was not yet clear to him. But when he returned to America,
he brought with him not only his own knowledge of music and
what the love of it could mean to an individual, but also a broad
and profound vision of what music could mean to a community
and to a nation. The implications of this vision were crucial to the
genesis of the Boston Symphony Orchestra.

Henry left Liverpool for Boston on November 17, 1860, eleven
days after Abraham Lincoln was elected President.

He returned to a country full of uncertainty. Six months later
Fort Sumter fell. It was with some relief that Henry immediately
participated in the formation of the Second Massachusetts Regi-
ment of Infantry, a group that naturally included his closest friends.
He was then transferred to the First Massachusetts Cavalry with a
captain's commission. Although he saw no battle in the infantry,
he knew much of the peripheral discomforts of being a soldier in a
badly managed war — no changes of clothes for six weeks and men
crying with hunger, for they had no regular meals for more than ten
days at a time. He also proved to be an able and capable officer.

At the beginning of the Battle of Aldie in June of 1863, Major
Higginson got into a skirmish with the enemy along the road. His
own words describe it best:

> In striking a man who was using improper language, I was knocked
> from my horse, and found myself in the road. Over me was stand-
> ing a man whom I had unhorsed, and who struck at my head. He
> then proposed to take me prisoner, but I told him I should die in a
> few minutes, for I put my hand under and found a hole in my

backbone. He took what he could get of my goods and rode off, leading my horse, which had been shot with four bullets.

Henry did not die. His horse was later recaptured and served as his riding horse for many years to come. The vagaries of civil war permitted an encounter one night, many years later, when Henry was having dinner with his son at the University Club in Boston. A Confederate officer, in Boston for the unveiling of a statue, came to their table and said pleasantly, "I want to see how good a job I did on your face that day at Aldie." Major Higginson gave him both hands and the two men talked until the small hours of the next morning.

Henry did have a saber cut in his face and a bullet in his spine, which was removed in Boston after his return. These injuries ended Henry's active service in the war. The Civil War left him with his six closest friends dead on its battlefields, and it was in their memory that he later gave property to Harvard for its athletic facilities. And ever after he preferred to be addressed with the rank he had earned: major.

In the autumn of 1863 Henry announced his engagement to Ida Agassiz, the sister of one of his closest friends and the daughter of Professor Agassiz at Harvard. They were married on December 5 in Harvard's Appleton Chapel.

Business then occupied his energies. Later in life he used to say, "Men often speak of me as successful in business, but I have guessed wrong more often than I have guessed right." His ventures in the next three years were two of these. The first was the result of an oil speculation, poorly conceived and badly managed. Henry was hired as an agent to the project in Pennsylvania. Slowly the project ground to a halt. Next he turned to ginning cotton in Georgia. His intention was to help the recently freed slaves by giving them jobs and a new life with dignity. He bought an estate formerly worked by slaves and after two years, in which poor crops resulted, he was forced to admit that the cotton had merely paid expenses and the former profit had come from selling slaves. He and his wife returned to Boston, where, on January 1, 1868, Henry became a partner in his father's brokerage firm, Lee, Higginson & Company. He stayed there until his death more than fifty years later.

In his later years Henry was first thought of as a patron of the arts and a public benefactor, but he was in fact a born merchant and happily remained so all his life. He loved adventure, particularly as it pertained to business. His job, simply stated, was to interest substantial investors in projects that ran considerable risks but, if successful, returned profits in the form of large fortunes.

There was ample business to be transacted at Lee, Higginson & Company. There was the sudden outpouring of stocks and bonds by the new western railroads, the postwar impetus of manufacturing industries, and speculation in gold and copper. The Calumet and Hecla Mine, which provided many, many fortunes, was a project of two of Henry's brothers-in-law. Henry helped his friends and relatives to establish some of the country's largest companies, including Bell Telephone and General Electric. Large fortunes were made — including Henry's.

The exact moment when Major Higginson conceived the idea of the Boston Symphony Orchestra is not known. He once said that it was during the winter of 1856 in Vienna. But even as a young adult he had enjoyed the various musical offerings in Boston.

In the forty years before the establishment of the orchestra, Boston's public had enjoyed concerts given by the country's oldest musical society, which still exists: the Handel and Haydn Society, formed in 1815. In the 1830s the Boston Music Academy was formed for educational purposes; the students gave concerts, and it was in their season of 1840–1841 that Boston first heard Beethoven's symphonies. The Harvard Musical Association was formed in 1837 by a group of alumni who wished to continue actively their interest in music. The guiding light of this private club was John S. Dwight, to whose *Journal of Music* young Henry Higginson contributed from Vienna. Although the association reflected Dwight's extreme conservatism in musical taste, it did much to promote concert music in Boston by sponsoring public concerts for the seventeen years immediately prior to the formation of the symphony. In addition to the classical works there were performances of more recent compositions, including the American première of Tchaikovsky's Piano Concerto no. 1. The association was in part responsible for the building of the Boston Music Hall in 1852. Visiting celebrities like Jenny Lind no longer had to perform in places as inappropriate

The Germania Musical Society in the 1840s.

as the Fitchburg railway station! The Germania Society, a fine orchestra from Germany, fled to America during the political upheavals of 1848 and toured the eastern part of the country for six years. It made frequent appearances in Boston, some with the Handel and Haydn Society, including a performance of Beethoven's Ninth Symphony. As an encore to one of its Music Hall concerts, the society played a piece called "The Railway Gallop," during which a small clockwork train went around and around the stage of the Music Hall sending out black cotton wool smoke! The Germania Society finally disbanded and its members settled in various cities, where they played an important part in the early efforts to organize and train local orchestras and choral societies.

The Theodore Thomas orchestra played more than two hundred concerts in Boston during the 1870s. Thomas, who was born in Germany, came to this country when he was fourteen, played in different bands, and was one of the early members of the New York Philharmonic Society. He took up conducting and with a missionary's zeal toured virtually every city east of the Mississippi; he did more to educate the widely spread American public to concert music than anyone of his generation. The core of his programs was the music of Beethoven, and with it he scheduled bright overtures, waltzes, and marches.

Major Higginson developed the plan for his orchestra in consultation with friends and with the advice of one of his former teachers in Vienna, Professor Julius Epstein. (Professor Epstein remained a close friend and valued adviser until his death after the First World War.)

Without prior announcement, this notice appeared in Boston's newspapers of March 30, 1881:

THE BOSTON SYMPHONY ORCHESTRA
In the Interest of Good Music

Notwithstanding the development of musical taste in Boston, we have never yet possessed a full and permanent orchestra, offering the best music at low prices, such as may be found in all the large European cities, or even in the smaller musical centres of Germany. The essential condition of such orchestras is their stability, whereas ours are necessarily shifting and uncertain, because we are dependent upon musicians whose work and time are largely pledged elsewhere.

To obviate this difficulty the following plan is offered. It is an effort made simply in the interest of good music, and though individual inasmuch as it is independent of societies or clubs, it is in no way antagonistic to any previously existing musical organization. Indeed, the first step as well as the natural impulse in announcing a new musical project, is to thank those who have brought us where we now stand. Whatever may be done in the future, to the Handel and Haydn Society and to the Harvard Musical Association we all owe the greater part of our home education in music of a high character. Can we forget either how admirably their work has been supplemented by the taste and critical judgment of Mr. John S. Dwight, or by the artists who have identified themselves with the same cause in Boston? These have been our teachers. We build on foundations they have laid. Such details of this scheme as concern the public are stated below.

The orchestra is to number sixty selected musicians; their time, so far as required for careful training and for a given number of concerts, to be engaged in advance.

Mr. George Henschel will be the conductor for the coming season.

The concerts will be twenty in number, given in the Music Hall on Saturday evenings, from the middle of October to the middle of March.

The price of season tickets, with reserved seats, for the whole series of evening concerts will be either $10 or $5, according to position.

Single tickets, with reserved seats, will be seventy-five cents or twenty-five cents, according to position.

Besides the concerts, there will be public rehearsal on one afternoon of every week, with single tickets at twenty-five cents, and no reserved seats.

The intention is that this orchestra shall be made permanent here, and shall be called 'The Boston Symphony Orchestra.'

Both as the condition and result of success the sympathy of the public is asked.

H. L. HIGGINSON

Chapter Two

The Early Conductors

"Without a certain amount of humility and a certain knowledge of
one's weaknesses and follies, how can anyone make any progress
in this world."
— Major Higginson

MAJOR HIGGINSON'S PLAN FOR A permanent resident orchestra
— with the musical direction and artistic decisions made by the
conductor and with musicians devoting the major part of their effort to the performance of symphonic music — became the foundation of later American orchestras. He also established the tradition
of private patronage for orchestras organized for the benefit of the
public. For this country, classical music has come to mean almost
exclusively music heard at symphony concerts. Consequently it
has become a matter of civic pride that a city or town, no matter
how small or remote, must have, along with its baseball team, its
own orchestra.

In 1976 there were more than 34 major orchestras, 92 metropolitan and regional orchestras, 50 urban, 440 college, 500 community,
and 255 youth orchestras, and 30 chamber orchestras. (These cate-
gories are designated by size of both budget and institution.)

Since the artistic and musical decisions of the Boston Symphony
have been made by its conductors, it is appropriate to follow its
story in relationship to them and to look briefly at the history of
conducting.

The art and profession of conducting has a surprisingly short
history of two hundred years, and its evolution continues. In earlier times, orchestras functioned under a divided leadership. The
orchestras of Handel and Mozart had a time beater, who beat time

from the keyboard instrument, and a leader, the first violin — now, the concertmaster — indicated soft or loud and generally kept things together. Today the divided leadership has reversed to the point where conductors divide their time between two orchestras often continents apart.

The concept of the orchestra — instruments accompanying instruments — is dependent on interpretation. Musical notation is an inexact language. The notes and the spaces between them are open to different readings. As the music of the nineteenth century evolved beyond the formal classical structure into a form that relied upon dynamic effects and varieties of subtle tone colors, conducting became overtly interpretative, and the art became a profession. The conductor of an orchestra is invariably also its music director, which means that he chooses what music will be performed. And it is on these choices and in the fulfillment of them that the success of a conductor and his orchestra rests.

The effects of the originality, sensitivity, and technique of a conductor become a powerful force in any community. It is he who represents music. So audiences are apt to feel strongly about conductors, as do musicians. They can tell from the first short trip from backstage to the podium whether or not their new conductor is a true leader and whether they will permit him to control their collective effort. They could give him their attention out of fear of his wrath, as it was with Muck and Koussevitzky, or out of respect and affection, as with Monteux and Munch.

The Boston Symphony Orchestra does not need a conductor in order to play Beethoven symphonies. They know the music well; most of the musicians have played those works literally hundreds of times. But they need the conductor to make that performance an important or even a great one. And that is the conductor's first duty: to inspire his musicians to play better than they think they can. Each must feel that he is expressing himself freely yet working together in a perfect ensemble.

After a particularly fine concert in Boston one day, an adoring lady told Koussevitzky that she sometimes thought he was God. He responded, "I know my responsibility." And he meant it. In many ways the conductor's relationship with his orchestra used to parallel a father-child relationship. Koussevitzky would tell the

Boston Symphony, "I am the father and you are my children," and no one but he spoke during rehearsals.

A description of a rehearsal in Leipzig in 1772 by the English music historian Dr.Charles Burney is interesting:

> The instrumental parts went ill; but this was the first rehearsal, they might have been disciplined into good order, if M. Hiller [the conductor] had chosen to bounce and play tyrant a little; for it is a melancholy reflection to make, that few composers [conductors] are well treated by an orchestra 'til they have first used the performers roughly, and made themselves formidable.

The degree and to what effect conductors have subsequently chosen to "bounce and play tyrant" have produced two hundred years of increasingly high standards for the performance of music, some spectacularly unforgettable concerts, and a host of conductor stories, some true.

There have been those such as Arthur Nikisch who never raised their voice. Bruno Walter treated his orchestra like highly esteemed colleagues. Others, like Arturo Toscanini, suffered when the musicians were unable to produce his vision of a work, and the ensuing temper was volcanic. It was a rare rehearsal when Toscanini did not stamp his feet and scream, casting aspersions on the players' paternity, mental competence, and physical completeness.

The day of the despotic conductor is ending. Many European orchestras are musicians' cooperatives, which control the choice not only of their conductor but also of their management. The last hundred years have seen a vast change in the professional and social status of musicians. Since the advent of the musicians' committees within orchestras and the national musicians' union, the players no longer fear the pernicious loss of their jobs and so no longer tolerate the abuses common in the past.

Jean Baptiste Lully's orchestra was the first example of a well-ordered instrumental ensemble under a single authority. His orchestra belonged to the court of Louis XIV, hence Lully's model for ruling was that of "The Mighty Personality." Lully was autocratic, arrogant, and the first of the great conductors. He was also conducting's first casualty. He conducted standing on a podium, using a heavy staff to beat time. In either a rage or ecstasy it struck his foot one day. The injury became gangrenous and Lully died. But his system worked and musicians, including Mozart, came from all over Europe to learn his technique.

In the eighteenth and early nineteenth centuries it was generally thought that the composer was the best person to conduct his own music. However, this was found to be not necessarily true. For example, Beethoven supervised many performances of his own music, with results that must have been a terrifying sight:

> Scarcely had the music begun before its creator offered a bewildering spectacle . . . at the *piano* passages he sank upon his knee, at the *forte* he leaped up; so that his figure, now shrivelling to that of a dwarf, disappeared under the desk, and anon stretched far above it like a giant, his hands and arms working as if with the beginning of the music a thousand lives entered every member.

As his deafness increased and his music became more complicated, the disaster multiplied. He would tell the orchestra not to play a repeat and then conduct it, including the repeat. The performance would slow to a halt as Beethoven yelled, "Stop! Stop! Wrong! That will not do! Again! Again!" Beethoven's deafness grew so bad that he could not hear the music around him, and audiences and musicians trembled when they knew he was to participate in a concert.

The conductor did not always stand on a podium facing his orchestra. In the performance of opera in the eighteenth and nineteenth centuries, the conductor invariably placed himself between the orchestra and the stage with his back to the orchestra. Further, until almost the turn of the twentieth century, musicians, with the exception of cellists, stood to play.

The use of the baton began in the 1820s. Louis Spohr is the first one to have used a baton rather than the time beater's staff. It must have been a small one, as he kept it in a pocket. It was also he who devised the system of letters attached to the score and its parts for easy reference during rehearsals. Berlioz's baton was described as "a cudgel of lime tree with the bark on." Mendelssohn's was a light stick of whalebone covered with white leather to match his white gloves. Most nineteenth-century conductors wore white gloves. The French conductor Louis Antoine Jullien, an unequaled showman who did more to educate nineteenth-century audiences to classical music in Europe than anyone else, was as exaggerated in his accouterments as he was bizarre in his fondness for outsized instruments and wild effects. He had a maple baton twenty-two inches long with chased gold circlets and entwined with two gold serpents with diamond eyes. He also had a huge velvet chair — one assumes red — set in the midst of the orchestra for himself should he need to rest. When he conducted Beethoven's music, his white gloves were presented to him on a silver tray.

All conductors must have good memories — some have been extraordinary — but conducting from memory is the personal preference of the conductor, and the importance attached to it means more to the public and press than to the conductor or musicians. Munch did not use a score for works he knew and loved well, but when he conducted contemporary music or there was a soloist he used a score and wore his glasses. Seiji Ozawa conducts from memory much of the time. When the score is in front of him, it invariably remains closed. In the time of Mendelssohn it was thought impolite not to use the score. One day the wrong score was placed in front of him; while he conducted from memory he turned the pages at what seemed appropriate intervals so that no one would be upset!

Hans von Bülow, a disciple of Wagner, was a great pianist and conductor. He presided over the best-trained and most well disciplined orchestra of the 1880s at Meiningen. But it took "ten hours of daily rehearsal! I am perfectly ruined and going to the dogs!" He did not, however, mention the musicians. Von Bülow was a disagreeable man who lectured audiences, put on black gloves to conduct the funeral march of the *Eroica*, and once played Beethoven's Ninth twice on the same program. Von Bülow learned everything by heart and demanded the same from his musicians. He once told his young pupil Richard Strauss, "You must have the score in your head, not your head in the score."

One of the first conductors who was not trained as a musical performer was Wagner, and he was reputed to be a poor score reader. But he, like Koussevitzky later, had an infallible intuitive sense and a blazing passion for music. He was one of the great conductors, and his approach to a performance was a creative one. He had a group of disciples (von Bülow was one), and they, with others of the later 1880s, extended their interpretations to include rewriting sections and changing the endings and the markings of the scores they conducted. This was done in the entirely good faith of self-expression and in the belief that the music was being modernized to be made more palatable to its listeners.

Toscanini was one of the very great conductors. He conducted from memory, but this was necessitated by his poor eyesight. Toscanini's approach was entirely different from the highly personal interpretations of those who had gone before him. For Toscanini all that mattered was the composer's markings and the notes themselves. "The tradition is found only in one place — the music," he said. And once he described his view of Beethoven's *Eroica:*

George Henschel, conductor of the BSO from 1881 to 1884.

"Some say it is Napoleon, some Hitler, some Mussolini. For me it is simply *Allegro con brio*." The intensity of his conducting and the demands for precision he made on his orchestra made his performances sound revolutionary and new. Toscanini was irritable and fearsome, heaping abuse on performers and hurling invectives at management, but his aims and aspirations for the performance of music are the dominating influence on the conductors of today.

Major Higginson chose as his first conductor George Henschel, whom he had heard conduct one of the concerts sponsored by the Harvard Musical Association. Henschel had started as a child prodigy who gave piano recitals in his native Germany at age

The Music Hall, first home of the orchestra, was built in 1852. It is pictured here in 1874.

Boston Music Hall

SEASON 1881-82.

BOSTON SYMPHONY ORCHESTRA

MR. GEORG HENSCHEL, Conductor.

I. CONCERT.

SATURDAY, OCTOBER 22D, AT 8, P. M.

PROGRAMME.

OVERTURE, Op. 124, "Dedication of the House."   BEETHOVEN.

AIR. (Orpheus.)   .   .   .   .   .   .   GLUCK.

SYMPHONY in B flat.   .   .   .   .   .   HAYDN.

(No. 12 of Breitkopf's edition.)

BALLET MUSIC. (Rosamunde.)   .   .   .   .   SCHUBERT.

SCENA. (Odysseus.)   .   .   .   .   .   MAX BRUCH.

FESTIVAL OVERTURE.   .   .   .   .   .   .   WEBER.

SOLOIST:

MISS ANNIE LOUISE CARY.

The first program of the first season, played Saturday, October 22, 1881.

twelve. He also had a very fine voice. In 1875 he sang the principal part in Bach's *Saint Matthew Passion,* conducted by Brahms. Henschel was also a composer, but it was his accomplishments as a singer and conductor that brought him success.

The summer before the orchestra's first season, Major Higginson commissioned Henschel to go to Europe and acquire a library of representative works by classical and modern composers. This initial collection formed the nucleus of the orchestra's now priceless library. Henschel himself catalogued and indexed each part and each work.

The orchestra was chosen, at Major Higginson's request, from local musicians, and rehearsals were held during the month prior to the first concert. Major Higginson stipulated that the concerts be short — an hour and a half instead of the four hours that European concerts lasted! Henschel structured the programs so that there were short opening works followed by the main work, either a symphony or a concerto. After the intermission there were some lighter works so that the audience could go home in a happy frame of mind. The program for the opening concert of Saturday, October 22, 1881, at the Boston Music Hall, was:

Overture, Op. 124 "Dedication of the House"	BEETHOVEN
Air (Orpheus)	GLUCK
Symphony in B Flat	HAYDN
Intermission	
Ballet Music (Rosamunde)	SCHUBERT
Scena (Odysseus)	MAX BRUCH
Festival Overture	WEBER

soloist
Miss Annie Louise Cary

The Boston Symphony concerts were an immediate, popular success. The establishment of the orchestra was an excitement, and no small part of this was the conductor himself.

George Henschel was a young man; he celebrated his thirty-second birthday during the first season. Although he was a musician of broad range with fine training, he had little experience or expertise as a conductor. He was respected by the musicians and had a temperament that provoked excitement and fire, which led one critic to point out, "Not that we object to fire, but we would rather be warmed by it than roasted in a furious conflagration."

Excitement and controversy are life's blood to a new project, and there was plenty of both during the first seasons. The concerts and their conductor were the topic of lively discussion by both audiences and the press. The controversy centered on Henschel's conducting techniques and also on his frequently scheduling his own compositions and duets to be sung by him and his wife. He also presented much contemporary music — works by Dvořák, Wagner, and his devoted friend Brahms. These works were not easily understood and not well received. According to the tradition of that time, a new work was often heard both at the beginning and at the end of the program.

But the programs of the first season also included, at Major Higginson's request, all nine of Beethoven's symphonies, with the Ninth concluding the season. Prior to the announcement of that concert, a notice appeared in the program: "Ladies and Gentleman desirous of singing in the chorus on that occasion, and willing to attend all the necessary rehearsals, are invited to write their names and addresses in a book provided for this purpose at Mr. Peck's

The first photograph of the Boston Symphony Orchestra, taken in 1882 during its first season in the Music Hall.

Mrs. George Henschel, formerly Lillian Bailey, with her husband. A soprano, she often sang with the orchestra.

office, Music Hall. The list will be made and ladies and gentlemen duly notified." Seven rehearsals were scheduled by Henschel and "Complimentary tickets can be given to the members of the chorus to the Public Rehearsal — March 21st — only!"

The concert was a great success and later Henschel wrote: "A great many people had to turn back and I myself in the Hall had difficulty to reach the conductor's desk, as every available space even on the platform was occupied by audience."

In the next seasons the conducting improved and even Henschel's most vehement critics subsided. The orchestra, working exclusively under one conductor, became the equal of if not better than any previously heard in Boston. The second season expanded to twenty-six concerts in Boston, six at Harvard, and several each in nearby towns. The orchestra also participated in various benefits and gave a special memorial concert to commemorate the death of Wagner in February 1883. The program was entirely devoted to Wagner's music, and in tribute the musicians wore black instead of the usual white neckties.

Henschel liked to include his audience as much as possible. He planned a concert celebrating the four hundredth birthday of Martin Luther and included as the final work Bach's *Ein Feste Burg*. The audience was asked to participate and sing the chorale with a large choir of boys from four different cities.

After three seasons the orchestra and its conductor had survived the initial problems inherent in any new project and, indeed, had established itself as Boston's permanent resident orchestra. Henschel, however, decided to resume his career of concert singing.

The orchestra was grateful to its first conductor and so was Boston. Henschel described his final concert:

> I shall never forget that last symphony concert I conducted in 1884. It was, to begin with, the Manfred Overture. I had just made the last touch of my baton to insure silence and raised it for the first sharp chord of the overture, when to my utter surprise and dismay, the whole audience rose to its feet and instead of hearing the Manfred Overture, my ears were bathed in a flow of "Auld Lang Syne" sung by a thousand people.

He was knighted in England after a most distinguished career,

Wilhelm Gericke, conductor of the orchestra, 1884–1889 and 1898–1906.

and as Sir George he returned to Boston in 1931 for the orchestra's fiftieth anniversary celebration. Although no member of the original orchestra sat onstage, two were in the audience, and Sir George conducted a concert almost identical to the one that had opened the first season.

Major Higginson frequently received compliments on his orchestra and much gratitude from the audiences, but when he was told that his orchestra was a great one he always answered that it was not yet but he hoped it would be in the future.

The orchestra's second conductor, Wilhelm Gericke, came from Vienna, where he had been conducting both the Vienna Court Opera and in the Opera House of Vienna. Although he was not yet forty when he arrived in Boston, he had had more than fifteen years' conducting experience in Linz and Vienna. He was a quiet, shy man, but he had an immediate and sustained success in Boston. A dignified, self-contained conductor, he was a pleasure to watch. His concerts were well received and the large drafty hall was frequently sold out. The audience was responsive and once even demanded an encore. A critic wrote:

> Boston auditors are beginning to recognize a good performance when they hear it . . . How different it used to be in Boston! I can remember concerts in the city where the critic felt very lonely . . . Of course in those days applause was unknown, and if once an enthusiastic youth did clap his hands, it was discovered that he came from New York . . .

Once the orchestra was established, Major Higginson was eager to raise the standards not only of performance but also of the programs themselves. The lighter works following the intermission were dropped, and the programs took on the character of true symphony concert.

Some of the audience did not adjust quickly. Gericke, like his predecessor, conducted performances of contemporary music. During the first performance of Brahms's Third Symphony the audience left the hall in hundreds. The same thing happened at the first performance of Richard Strauss's *In Italy* (1888). During the last movement of the first performance of Bruckner's Symphony no. 7 (1887), there were more people on the stage than in the audience. The symphony was described by the critic of the *Saturday Evening Gazette* as "a prolonged moan and groan, varied now and then with a gloomy and soul depressing bellow; Wagner in a prolonged attack of sea-sickness; a huge barnacle covered whale of a symphony but without any lubricating blubber." Another suggested that in case of fire Bruckner's Seventh should be played so that the hall would empty instantly.

Gericke, by his own account, had a very difficult first year. After the second concert he told Major Higginson, "There are some musicians, but it is hardly an orchestra." He was a cool, relentless drillmaster and disciplinarian. The orchestra was not used to his way of rehearsing or the demands he made upon it, and by the end of his first season many of the orchestra members had left.

A six-month season was certainly not long enough to insure that a musician would return after the lean summer months. Major Higginson and Gericke proposed a longer season of eight or nine months, including visits to other cities. They also devised the plan for the Popular, or Pops, concerts for several weeks at the start of summer, which would extend the season and offer a new opportunity for the city to enjoy music. In this way they hoped that contracts for several years could be offered to the musicians and provide continuity for the orchestra.

When twenty musicians needed to be replaced at the end of Gericke's first season, he went to Europe to find them. All the new musicians he brought back were young, and one of the youngest

The Franz Kneisel Quartet, also supported by Major Higginson.

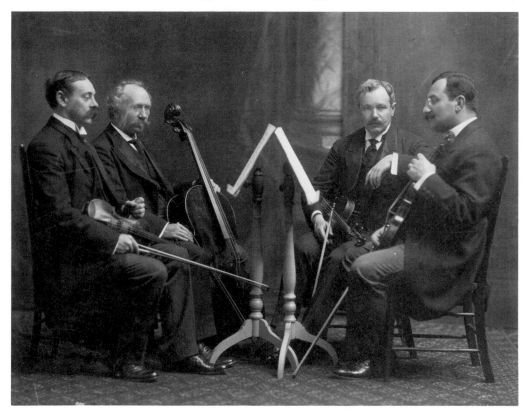

Arthur Nikisch, conductor of the BSO, 1889–1893.

was the new concertmaster, Franz Kneisel, who remained with the orchestra for eighteen years and only resigned in order to devote his time to the chamber concerts of his famous Kneisel Quartet. On the trip to America he was, as Gericke described him, "so young that he did not even know how to smoke. On our trip over, I felt it my duty to teach him this art, in which he has certainly been past-master ever since."

By the middle of Gericke's second season, the musicians began to realize the benefits of their hard work and grueling training. In Philadelphia they earned their first out-of-town success. At the end of Gericke's third season the orchestra went to New York and was well received and highly acclaimed. Even then success in New York was what mattered. It was not until then that the musicians, their conductor, and Major Higginson knew they were part of an artistic organization of the first rank.

The Boston Symphony was begun under Henschel, but it truly established itself under Gericke's baton. In his final season the orchestra played one hundred and twelve concerts to audiences averaging twenty-five hundred each, and at the end of the regular season they made a tour west as far as St. Louis. On their return to Boston, Gericke bid the orchestra farewell and at the end of the testimonial farewell concert "the audience rose . . . and shouted themselves hoarse, while waving of hats and handkerchiefs was carried on even by the most sedate individuals."

Arthur Nikisch came to Boston in 1889, when he was thirty-four. Born in Hungary in 1855, he had been a child prodigy, giving his first piano recital at age eight. He also had an extraordinary musical memory, and at age seven he was able to write down, note for note, the Overture to Rossini's *William Tell* after hearing it just once. At eleven he became a student at the Vienna Conservatory. He so distinguished himself in his entrance examination that he was placed in the highest class with pupils twice as old as he. He studied the violin and at age thirteen won the conservatory's great gold medal for the composition of a chamber work, the first prize for violin playing, and the second prize for piano! In May 1872 he was among the first violins in the historical performance of Beethoven's Ninth Symphony at the stone-laying ceremonies of the Bayreuth Festspielhaus, conducted by Wagner. He also played violin in an orchestra in Vienna under such conductors as Anton Rubinstein, Liszt, Brahms, and Wagner. In his early twenties, Nikisch became conductor of the opera in Leipzig and led orchestral concerts, too, including a performance of Schumann's D Minor Symphony after which he was congratulated by the composer's widow, Clara.

Nikisch was the embodiment of the romantic conductor. He was a small handsome man with lots of hair and a well-manicured beard. He liked his shirts to have large collars and enormous cuffs in order to emphasize his delicate hands. Not a learned or intellectual man, he preferred music, cards, and women. No one ever saw him lose his temper, and his most severe words to his orchestra were "Will you kindly . . ." or "Excuse me but . . ."

His training and early experience having been in the performance of music, he understood musicians and orchestras loved him. Where some conductors need many hours or even months to get an orchestra to play the way they want, Nikisch would do so at the first rehearsal. The description of a Nikisch rehearsal of the London Symphony Orchestra says much about the Nikisch style. One day in 1905 the orchestra had had a morning rehearsal with another conductor, an afternoon concert, and a rehearsal with Nikisch that was due to begin at 7:00 P.M. Needless to say, the men were tired and angry. The work to be rehearsed was Tchaikovsky's Fifth Symphony. One of the musicians wrote:

> Before we had been playing five minutes we were deeply interested and, later, when we came to the big *fortissimos* we not only played like fiends but forgot we were tired. The weird part of it all was that we played the Symphony through — with scarcely a word of direction from Herr Nikisch — quite differently from our several performances of the same work. He simply *looked* at us, often scarcely moving his baton, and we played as those possessed.

Tchaikovsky himself wrote after a concert:

> Herr Nikisch [is] quiet, sparing of superfluous movements, and yet so extraordinarily commanding, powerful, full of self control . . . This conductor is small in stature, a very pale young man with splendid poetical eyes that really must possess mesmeric powers.

Evidently they did.

After he had conducted the opera orchestra at La Scala, Nikisch complimented the young Toscanini on its fine quality. Toscanini knew better: "I happen to know this orchestra very well. I am the conductor of this orchestra. It is a bad orchestra. You are a good conductor." No wonder orchestras loved to play for him. He was not aware of how he achieved his results. His was a highly personal performance and, like Wagner and others of his time, he retouched scores in order "to bring out the real intentions of the master." Nikisch's baton technique was innovative. He did not hold it, as others did, in his fist but lightly between two fingers and thumb so that it became an extension of his fingers and hand rather than of his shoulder. He used a light, long stick, and he used his left hand independently and more than other conductors of his time. Another Nikisch innovation, now taken for granted, was that he beat a fraction of a second in advance of the music instead of with it.

Nikisch came to Boston; later Major Higginson looked back and wrote:

> I had known about Mr. Nikisch from my Viennese friends, and was quite aware of his high quality. He came in the autumn of 1889, and immediately took up his work with great energy. He was, I think, surprised to find how good the orchestra was . . . but he put into it all his power, passion, and wonderful skill in producing results, and he gave us very different effects from Mr. Gericke. He was a man of real genius.

When Nikisch first heard the Boston Symphony he was delighted — "All I have to do is poetize." And for four years he and the orchestra did just that.

Nikisch became a craze in Boston. What people thought of him was the topic of constant and fervid discussion. A music critic in New York noted: "The conductor cult is a phase of social activity which flourishes only in Boston." Whatever people thought of him, he continued to establish the favor of the orchestra with an ever-extending public. The concerts on what was known as the "southern" trips to New York, Philadelphia, and Baltimore were sold out, and of the three thousand patrons at the first Philadelphia concert in 1893, seven hundred and fifty were standees.

Nikisch's first concern was for the highly personal performance of music. Major Higginson's was in the establishment and sustenance of a first-class orchestra. That the two men got along so well for four years was a tribute to both. The other side of relying on intuition and mesmerism, no matter how well it works, is laziness. Nikisch often did not open the score of a new work until its first rehearsal. Although the performance might be fine, the orchestra itself lacked the hard, day-to-day routine and the general, if not rigid, discipline that must be present for an orchestra to play its best.

At the time of the Chicago World's Fair of 1893, the Boston Symphony Orchestra played but was conducted by its concertmaster, Franz Kneisel, due to some misunderstanding about the specifics of Nikisch's contract. Major Higginson remained unmesmerized and Nikisch returned to Europe. There he continued his extraordinary, dynamic career as one of the very greatest conductors.

At that point Major Higginson sent his friend O. W. Donner to

Vienna to find, in consultation with Professor Epstein and Gericke, a new conductor for the orchestra. A Wagner disciple, Hans Richter, one of the most important conductors in Europe, did sign a contract but was ultimately unable to secure his release from his contract in Vienna. Richter was a difficult man. Donner complained in a letter to Major Higginson: "You told me at the time that artists were a 'queer lot,' but in Richter's case this is much too mild an expression." Gericke's health was not good enough for him to return at that time, so several other conductors were invited, and finally Emil Paur was chosen.

Paur was a contemporary of Nikisch and, like him, had been a child prodigy, studying first with his father, the director of a musical society. He performed on the violin and piano in public at age eight and studied composition and violin at the Vienna Conservatory. Paur began his conducting career when he was twenty-one and succeeded Nikisch at Leipzig when the latter came to Boston in 1889. Paur was a romantic conductor typical of his time. Boston

Emil Paur, conductor of the BSO, 1893–1898.

critics praised his robustness and his sincerity, and he stayed for five years. He was an energetic conductor who evidently stamped his feet for emphasis. The music critic of the *Journal* wrote:

> Mr. Paur would certainly be horrified if he knew that his habit disturbed anyone prepared to admire him. The habit if unconscious is probably confirmed. Now what shall be done? . . . Why should not Mr. Paur be presented with a pair of thick fur boots with felt soles? . . . Rubber boots are cheaper; but they would chafe the conductor in his more impassioned moments; they yield an unsavory smell; they have a cold, wet noise of their own, even when they are perfectly dry.

Paur was open to new musical ideas, and he continued the tradition established by his predecessors of bringing new works to his audiences, particularly the large works of Richard Strauss and Brahms. It was just fifteen years since audiences had fled Brahms's First Symphony under Gericke; now they stayed to applaud. In April of 1896 there was a memorial to Brahms, who had died a week earlier, at which his Fourth Symphony was performed.

Unlike his predecessors, Paur did not immediately return to Europe after his appointment in Boston was concluded. He went to New York and replaced Anton Seidl at the Philharmonic.

Later Paur wrote about his stay in Boston and about the orchestra. It is a significant document that captures much of the essence and detail of Major Higginson's project.

> Great was my delighted surprise and astonishment when I heard the Boston men at my first rehearsal! I found an excellent assembly of musicians of the first rank who did not play only to do their duty and satisfy the conductor and audience; they played in the heart and soul, joy and enthusiasm, inclined always to give their very best and cooperate with the conductor to reach the highest possible perfection. It is the best orchestra in the world, that was my conviction which I had when I started my work in Boston, and which conviction has not changed since then.
>
> The institution of the Boston Symphony Orchestra is "unique." In the whole world, one could not find a man who would spend a great fortune to educate the people of a great country musically, in founding an orchestra equipped with the best musicians to be had, under the leadership of an unsurpassed manager and a best-known

Standing in line for tickets at the Music Hall in the 1890s.

musical conductor. The reason why the Boston Orchestra plays better than all other existing orchestras is — besides the excellent qualities of the men — the comfortable living the men are able to enjoy. They all are paid better than anywhere else, consequently they have no sorrow of provisions; they feel free, satisfied, happy, not overworked, and the result is joy, enthusiasm, and perfection in their work. There are other wisest points in the rules set by the founder of the Boston Orchestra, which brought the institution to the best in the world. The most important and wisest one is the absolute power given to the manager, in all business matters, and to the conductor in all artistic, musical matters, both *only* responsible to the owner of the Orchestra.

The response of the people in the period of my conductorship, 1893–98, was, in spite of the very bad business time, growing from year to year in regard to attendance and understanding. It was a great delight to me to see and feel the rise of true and warm love and enthusiasm for great masters like Brahms, Liszt, Wagner, Tschaykowski, R. Strauss, and others. In the first years of the existence of the Orchestra it was necessary to engage great soloists for the concerts to attract the people; my predecessor and I began to reduce the number of concerts with soloists every year more and more, and it proved to be right.

The people nowadays fill the concerts of the Symphony Orchestra, not on account of the soloist, but only on account of the masterful playing of great musical works. The people in Boston know what they have, and love and appreciate gratefully the ideal thing which Major Higginson has nobly given them. The wonderful institution means an everlasting monument to the unselfish founder, who not even wanted to have his name publicly connected with his great institution.

The five years I have spent in Boston count to the happiest years of my life. I never will and never could forget my days in Boston, thanks to the highly admired Major Higginson, the Bostonians, and the wonderful Boston Orchestra.

Ever since its first performance, the concerts of the Boston Symphony had been held in the big, drafty Music Hall on Hamilton Place. In the 1890s there was a plan to put a road through Hamilton Place, which would mean demolishing the old Music Hall.

During the next few years there was much interest and excitement in the planning of what was to be Symphony Hall.

An architect's drawing of the new music hall, which was called Symphony Hall.

A view of Symphony Hall in the 1960s.

Chapter Three

Symphony Hall

"A man may not undertake a real job and then drop it, to ease himself . . . I will not sin against our country's welfare, or even disregard well-founded complaints of my loyalty. No one ever alleges anything overt, but some good people snarl."
— Major Higginson

AT THE TURN OF THE CENTURY the southwest section of Boston began to expand in a special way. Six large buildings were built specifically to house and to serve cultural institutions.

Symphony Hall was the first to be completed, with its inaugural concert taking place in the fall of 1900. Horticultural Hall, just across the street, opened in 1903 (although it was begun earlier than Symphony Hall). The Museum of Fine Arts was rapidly enlarging its collections, and it moved from its orginal home in Copley Square to its present building on the Fenway. The New England Conservatory was built in 1902, including its small concert hall (Jordan Hall), and the Opera House opened in 1909. Fenway Court, later known as the Isabella Stewart Gardner Museum, was not then open to the public, but it was built at that time, too, and had a festive opening in 1903 that featured members of the Boston Symphony Orchestra.

These buildings and their endowed institutions were the gifts of successful and proud residents of Boston who had visited the great cultural centers of Europe and wished to communicate the results of their own success and good fortune to others in their city. This was before personal and corporate income tax and tax-deductible donations, so these were substantial, outright gifts to the community that reflected the current philosophy as simply stated by Major

Higginson: "To the more fortunate people of our land belongs the privilege of providing the higher branches of education and of art."

In order to finance Symphony Hall, a corporation was formed and stock sold. The total cost of the building was $750,000; to raise the entire amount the building was mortgaged and on its completion leased to Major Higginson, who absorbed the expenses "of administration, taxes and all charges."

The financial responsibilities that Major Higginson assumed were staggering. From 1881 until 1918 the musicians had individual contracts with Major Higginson. The conductors' contracts were also personal contracts, as was that of the manager, Charles Ellis. Major Higginson was therefore not only the generous founder of an institution; his was the personal tangible commitment for its immediate and continuing sustenance. Since the money involved — and it was a large sum — had to be earned each year, his burden must at times have seemed overwhelming. And there were moments when, given the inevitable frictions within the orchestra or community, he thought of abandoning the project, especially when times were difficult financially. Once or twice he came close to bankruptcy, so quietly and anonymously Henry's brother Francis, a successful broker in New York, took over full responsibility for his brother's obligations. When Major Higginson did consider abandoning the project, the ideals of his own profound commitment to music, to education, and to his country dictated that he continue. His views of the requisites of the orchestra were:

> to leave the choice and care of the musicians, the choice and care of the music, the rehearsals and direction of the orchestra to the conductor, giving him every power possible; to leave to an able manager the business affairs of the enterprise; and on my part, to pay the bills, to be satisfied with nothing short of perfection . . .

Major Higginson maintained complete control over the design and building of Symphony Hall. The architects were McKim, Mead, and White, who were among the most prestigious of their time. Their original design for the new building was for a semicircular auditorium based on the design of a Greek theater, then in fashion. This plan was discarded by Major Higginson because the acoustics of such a hall were unpredictable. He hired Professor

Wallace C. Sabine, an assistant professor of physics at Harvard, to work with the architects, thereby making Symphony Hall the first hall in the world to be built in conformity with acoustical laws. The design and proportion of Symphony Hall are based on that of the Leipzig Gewandhaus, whose projection of sound is glorious. It is not possible to reconstruct an exact acoustical copy of an auditorium. However, Professor Sabine and the architects, working closely with the conductor, managed to combine the best of the Leipzig Gewandhaus and the old Music Hall. Symphony Hall seats 2625, one thousand more than the Gewandhaus and two hundred more than the old Music Hall. The loudness, interference, resonance, and reverberation of the music were all carefully and scientifically tested in the building's planning. The results are now well known: Symphony Hall is the most acoustically beautiful auditorium in this country and considered one of the great ones of the world. The hall is rectangular, with two wraparound balconies.

The interior of Symphony Hall.

The statues above the second balcony serve an acoustical as well as aesthetic purpose. There are twenty-one doors to the auditorium, and on each is the sign EXIT — not as someone in the planning stages suggested: THIS WAY OUT IN CASE OF BRAHMS.

Until the day of the first concert, the name of the new building was a well-kept secret. The reason for this is not clear, but evidence of it is seen in the letters BMH in the iron medallions of the banisters on each of the main staircases. The architect must have assumed that the building would be called the new Boston Music Hall. Nowhere on its exterior are there any words at all.

Wilhelm Gericke returned to Boston for a second term as conductor. It was appropriate that he, who had done so much to establish the quality of the orchestra, should conduct the first concert in the new hall on October 15, 1900. It was a gala occasion. The main work was a performance of Beethoven's *Missa Solemnis* with the Cecilia Society. Major Higginson welcomed the audience in a short speech from the stage, in which he began by describing the building of the hall and ended by thanking the orchestra and its conductor: "I am very proud of him and of them, this band of artists and I again thank them with all my heart, for they have done our city and our country signal and intelligent service, such as ennobles a nation." The opening of the new hall was the occasion for a public show of appreciation to Major Higginson. Hundreds of letters arrived thanking him for his generosity. A group of friends commissioned a bust by Saint-Gaudens. However, the sculptor was not well, so it was made later by Bela Pratt (1911); it still stands in the foyer of Symphony Hall: "A Tribute to the Founder and Sustainer of the Boston Symphony Orchestra."

The orchestra's method of selling tickets was unique. When the tickets went on sale for the first season in September of 1881, there was an enormous demand for them. They went on sale at 6:00 A.M. and seventy-five people were in line, some having been there all night and one even from 3:00 P.M. the previous day. The first man in line reputedly sold his position for $35! Since the demand for tickets was so high the practice of scalping became prevalent, so Major Higginson proposed a more equitable method. Thus in the third season the seats were put up for auction, and this notice, from Henry L. Higginson, appeared in the press: "The seats will be offered in regular succession according to their place on the plan, and not in order of superiority nor will the right to select be offered . . . From one to four seats as desired, may be bought on one bid. Bids must be made in person or by an agent."

The bids were premiums added to the regular price. The auctions started at 10:00 A.M. and continued until 6:45 in the evening, with half an hour for lunch. When the auction was finished the remaining tickets went on sale in the box office. The auctioning of tickets lasted thirty years, and there was always great interest and curiosity to see who would pay the most. Often it was Mrs. Jack Gardner, a friend of Major Higginson and a rabid Red Sox fan. On occasion she came late to concerts directly from Fenway Park, wearing a hat with a red band around it that read: O YOU RED SOX.

Some two hundred and fifty-one seats on the second balcony are kept as rush seats, available only to those who wait in line on the day of the concert. Major Higginson's purpose in selling these seats this way was to give students and others who could not afford or did not want a full season's subscription the opportunity to hear individual concerts. Initially the cost of each seat, one to a person, was 25 cents; now, almost one hundred years later, they are only $1.50 and still one to a person.

During the second season Major Higginson brought in a staff member from Lee, Higginson & Company to be the manager of the orchestra. Charles Ellis thus became the first full-time manager of an orchestra in this country, and his personal style of self-efface-ment set the standard for that role for many years. He acted as Major Higginson's deputy with tact and kindness in all matters concerning the orchestra's day-to-day functioning both at home and on trips to other cities.

In the early seasons Ellis quickly established that the orchestra was a serious, professional organization. Until then, and probably with good reason, soloists appearing with orchestras insisted that they be paid in advance. Ellis stopped that custom. He also re-fused to permit the piano companies to hang large advertisements on the side of the solo instrument on stage. Since then, a note of grateful acknowledgment in the program suffices.

Not all of management's problems were that straightforward. In

1888 the orchestra made a tour to central New York State; from an article in *Harper's Weekly* written somewhat later this appears:

> Arriving in town with the Orchestra for a concert that night, Comee [the assistant manager] went direct to the theatre to see what the sale was, that being the most important question of the day. He was greeted by the local manager with that calm indifference assumed when the house is rented and the money is sure, whether or not any tickets are sold. The advance sale was discouraging, and Comee turned to the local manager for comfort and suggestion. "When do you parade?" asked the local man. "Parade?" queried Comee in a puzzle. "Sure. Don't your troupe always parade before the show? You won't do business without it."
>
> And the impresario was right.

At home in Boston there was cause for excitement. In the programs of the 1908 season the ladies were amazed to note the announcement that in the city of Boston a revised regulation prohibited "any person to wear upon the head a covering which obstructs the view of the exhibition or performance." An emissary went to Ellis to ask what he intended to do. He gallantly answered, "The gracious women with musical taste can be depended upon to wear hats, if they wear any, against which the meanest man on earth could find no indictment." However, the women with musical taste were defiant. This, after all, was the time of the Merry Widow vogue, and hats were not only large but spectacular. On October 29, 1908, management announced that hats would be held in the lap during concerts or checked at the door. Only Isabella Stewart Gardner and five others were defiant. But their numbers increased in the next weeks. Mayor John F. Fitzgerald wrote from city hall that the license of Symphony Hall to operate as a meeting place would be revoked and the ladies had until November 19 to submit! On that day it must have seemed to Ellis that an extra large number of particularly spectacular hats were being paraded in the corridors. The ladies were duly warned. One asked for her money back, got it, and left. One said that if she took her hat off it would be impossible to put it back on again, so she was permitted to attend the concert standing with her back to a wall. Finally, the last bell rang, and at the penultimate moment the hats came off and the concert began.

Ellis managed not only the Boston Symphony but also several individual artists of international standing, among them Fritz Kreisler, Paderewski, and Geraldine Farrar. At one moment in his career he was offered the job of managing the Metropolitan Opera Company in New York at many times his Boston salary. Major Higginson simply said, "But I can't run the orchestra without you, Charlie." And so Charlie stayed in Boston.

During Gericke's second period with the orchestra, from 1889 to 1906, there were some significant changes and a further establishment of the orchestra within the community. First, of course, was the building of Symphony Hall, giving the orchestra its own home. Even though it had been discussed for several years, a plan for a

Charles Ellis, the first full-time manager of an orchestra in this country. He administered the BSO from 1882–1918.

Karl Muck in 1906. He conducted the BSO from 1906
to 1908 and from 1912 to 1918.

pension fund for the musicians had never been established. At
Gericke's insistence it was set up, and the annual pension fund
concerts, its primary source of income, began in 1903. Richard
Strauss conducted his own music at the Pension Fund Concert of
1904. He was enormously impressed with the orchestra and
wished he could have it in Europe to perform all the Beethoven
symphonies. Sir George Henschel, the orchestra's first conductor,
returned to conduct a Beethoven overture in the concert of 1905.

In 1901 Philip Hale, one of Boston's respected music critics, was
invited to edit the program book, which had formerly been the
target of his scorn. It soon became a most effective educational
medium for the orchestra.

Several key players of the orchestra resigned in the early 1900s.
The most significant loss was the concertmaster of eighteen years,
Franz Kneisel, who with three others formed the Kneisel Quartet
and wished to devote all their energies to it. Charles Loeffler, then
just a budding composer and violinist in the orchestra, also resigned

in order to concentrate on composing. Three French players were lost at sea on their way to a holiday in France.

The music played during Gericke's second term began by being traditional and conservative. Gradually it broadened considerably to include contemporary works that had not been heard in Boston before. These included Brahms's First Piano Concerto, Mahler's Fifth Symphony, Rachmaninoff's First Piano Concerto, Sibelius's Second Symphony, works by Debussy and Fauré, and a memorial concert for Dvořák. The French composer Vincent d'Indy was invited to conduct several concerts, including a preseason tour. Beginning in Canada, the tour also included Detroit and cities in northern New York State where orchestras had never been heard. In Boston d'Indy offered a program of his own modern French music as well as that of Fauré, Franck, and Dukas. The audience received the music well, but as a little-known critic wrote: "It was music, but as a Beacon Street ghost once said of the Hereafter, 'It wasn't Boston.' " This was a time when nearly every concert included a soloist of international renown, including Fritz Kreisler, de Pachmann, Gabrilowitsch, Bauer, Paderewski, and Eugène Ysaye.

When Gericke resigned at the end of the 1905–1906 season, a benefit concert was given at which the much-loved conductor received gifts of both money and silver objects. The event was described in a newspaper as a "Big Family Party," and Boston showed its indebtedness to the conductor who had been with the orchestra for thirteen of its twenty-five years and who, more than

Muck with the orchestra on the stage of Symphony Hall.

anyone else, had trained it and brought it to a level comparable to that of any of the great orchestras in Europe. Gericke received praise from the national press on the consistently high quality of programs and performance and his retirement was regretted. A reporter in Cleveland wrote: "In Boston the leader of the orchestra is a good deal bigger man than the mayor."

Karl Muck was the conductor of the orchestra for the two years from 1906 to 1908. In his middle forties when he came, he was a highly educated man, having earned his Doctor of Philosophy at the universities in Leipzig and Heidelberg. Muck made his debut as a pianist at the Gewandhaus in 1880. Shortly thereafter, he turned to conducting and held positions in Salzburg, Brno, Graz, and Prague. In 1892 he became Kapellmeister at the Royal Opera in Berlin, leaving it to come to Boston in 1906. Muck also conducted at the Bayreuth Festival in 1902. Since the Royal Opera was under the direct patronage of the emperor, imperial consent was needed for him to leave. This was obtained for one and then another year.

Muck's first concert was the twenty-four hundredth in the orchestra's history. It included works by Wagner and Beethoven — and he paid the orchestra the great compliment during the Beethoven symphony of laying down his baton and letting the music unfold.

His method of programming was quite different from those of the conductors before him. His concerts always had a variety to them in terms of period and nationality or mood and style. Soloists had to fit in with the overall musical plan of the concert, and Muck used fewer than had been common. In addition to the standard German repertory, he also conducted Debussy's *La Mer* in its Boston première and Sibelius's First Symphony. At the end of his first season a list of works performed was compiled, which showed the classical and modern works to be almost equal in number. Perhaps the most interesting aspect of the list is that Wagner and Brahms came under the heading of classics. Muck was a most skillful accompanist. However, he did not like to be kept waiting. Once Paderewski took longer to emerge from his dressing room than necessary. The audience, orchestra, and conductor all waited. Finally Muck strode to the stage door and, for all to hear, said, "Tell the king of Poland I am waiting for him."

At the end of two seasons Muck was denied an extension of his leave by Kaiser Wilhelm and so returned to Berlin. It was hoped that Gustav Mahler might come to Boston; he was then conducting opera in New York. He could not, but he recommended Willem Mengelberg and in a letter to him wrote: "The Boston position is the finest imaginable for a musician. An orchestra of the first rank. Unlimited sovereign power. A social standing such as the musician cannot obtain in Europe. A public of whose keenness to learn and whose gratitude the European can form no conception."

But Mengelberg also could not come, so Muck suggested his friend Max Fiedler from Hamburg.

After a benefit concert, Muck left Boston. Louis Elson, a music critic, wrote: "For the zeal our conductor has always displayed in advancing the cause of American music, for the brilliancy with which he has taught us new points even in familiar works, for the faithfulness with which he has sustained the high standard of our Symphony concerts, we lift up 'the still, small voice of Gratitude.' "

Max Fiedler, an exact contemporary of Muck, was both a conductor and composer. After studying piano at the Leipzig Conservatory, he joined the staff of the Hamburg Conservatory and became its director in 1904; he also led Hamburg's Philharmonic concerts. Max Fiedler's training represents an interesting step in the evolution of the profession of conducting. Whereas Henschel, Gericke, Nikisch, Paur, and Muck had all received their training in the opera house, Fiedler was the first to have received his in the concert hall. In 1905 he was the guest conductor of the New York Philharmonic and in 1907, of the London Symphony Orchestra. It was also the first time since Henschel that the conductor of the Boston Symphony spoke fluent English.

Fiedler did not continue Muck's philosophy of unit programs; rather, he sought to entertain and please with variety and contrast. The music critic H. T. Parker wrote: "He is hardly a conductor for connoisseurs, he is a conductor to please the general public." He was a most vigorous conductor, and the young Olin Downes, in the lush prose of the times, said, "He shook with galvanic fury, and the instruments vomited blasts of heaven-storming tone."

During Fiedler's four years in Boston Sergei Rachmaninoff was a visitor and with the orchestra played his F-sharp Minor Concerto.

Max Fiedler conducted the orchestra between Muck's terms, from 1908 to 1912.

He also conducted his symphonic poem *The Rocks*. He was described as a "pianist of marked ability and a conductor of unusual skill, authority and magnetism." His Second Symphony was also performed in Boston at that time. Fiedler's taste was eclectic. He conducted Tchaikovsky's *Nutcracker Suite* — its first performance in the orchestra's history (it had been given its American première at the Pops concerts before the turn of the century).

The opening concert of the 1910–1911 season commemorated the centennial of Schumann's birthday. Fiedler conducted the first performance in Boston of Scriabin's *Poem of Ecstasy*. One critic noted that "some of this ecstasy was extremely bitter." Fiedler had become a friend of Richard Strauss and played much of his music. He also reinstated the brilliant array of the reigning soloists of the day: the singers Madame Schumann-Heink and Geraldine Farrar; the violinists Fritz Kreisler, Mischa Elman, and Efrem Zimbalist; and the pianists Paderewski, Josef Hofmann, Rachmaninoff, and Ferruccio Busoni. Boston was described by Busoni in a letter to his wife as "Dear Old Boston," and he noted that it was much the same as it had been in 1892 and "almost a second Vienna." He went on to portray it as a town of inherited traditions and with affection described the elderly waitresses in glasses who made him feel as if he were in a hospital.

Fiedler left Boston in 1912 at the end of a buoyant leadership that was clearly marked by his enthusiasms and his attention to the contemporary works of French, Russian, English, and American composers.

At the same time, Muck received imperial permission to return to Boston, this time for five years. During his absence from Boston he had been honored by the emperor with the title General Musical Director, which was simultaneously awarded to Richard Strauss. This high honor had been given only three times in the previous two hundred years, to Spontini, Meyerbeer, and Mendelssohn.

Though not a pleasant man, Muck was a superb music director and conductor. The orchestra under his ever demanding, refining hand became world-famous for the astonishing, consistent beauty of its performances. There are those, like composer Roger Sessions, who believe the orchestra reached its greatest heights under Muck. He was hard-working and conscientious. He spent a great deal of time and care in the preparation of his programs and in their rehearsal. On the podium he had a very clear beat without mannerisms and he always had the score in front of him. His concept of music was not the highly personal, interpretative one of those before him; rather, his interest was in the structure of the composition just as the composer had written it. He did not like Tchaikovsky's music but was passionately fond of Mahler's and Bruckner's.

In this period he introduced works by Sibelius and Debussy and conducted the American première of Schönberg's Five Pieces for Orchestra. Afterward he remarked, "I can't tell you whether we've played music but I assure you we've played every one of Schönberg's notes, just as they were written."

In 1914 war was declared in Europe. In the United States there were terrible tensions and a mounting hysteria concerning all things even remotely German. In New York the German Hospital became the Lenox Hill Hospital. The Metropolitan Opera dropped the performance of its German repertoire. Hamburgers were no longer hamburgers — they were libertyburgers. And the hysteria grew into a witch hunt. Arthur Fiedler, conductor of the Boston Pops, was then in his late teens and a violinist in the orchestra. A native American (and not related to conductor Max Fiedler), he had trained in Berlin, played under Muck at the Berlin Opera, and joined the Boston Symphony in 1915. He remembers those days vividly and with sadness. He and a friend shared a house in Rockport, right on the water. He recalled, "You could spit into the sea from it." On the porch they had festive Japanese lanterns. One night U.S. marshals arrived and accused them of signaling to U-boats reputedly nearby. Young Arthur loved the dark rye bread then sold only in delicatessens. But he soon found that between the oven and his table it always bore the marks of a long hat pin seeking out its "enemy messages." Local children nudged each other and snickered, pointing to "the German spy."

This was a time of terrible harassment, and many were victims of slander that was sanctified by the piety of patriotism at low ebb. As the war continued in Europe, Muck, wearing the tie pin given to him by Emperor Wilhelm II, conducted the concerts of the Boston Symphony. Major Higginson, a proud patriot, found himself

in an impossible situation. His life's work had been to found and
to sustain a great orchestra for the benefit of his fellow citizens and
his country. The orchestra's foundation was deeply rooted in the
noble German-Austrian musical tradition. Many of its musicians
and all of its conductors had been chosen expressly because they
were exponents of that living tradition. The great orchestral music
of the time was German. High above center stage at Symphony
Hall, inscribed in the ornate crest, is the name Beethoven. Major
Higginson had a personal responsibility to the musicians, twenty-
two of whom were German; others, French and Belgian, could not
have gone home even had they wanted to. The indomitable old
man — he was nearly eighty — still lived by his own belief that
"education is the object of man." He believed that there was one
more lesson to be learned and that he and his orchestra might teach
it: that war and music are separate. Noting that "the passions of
men have been inflamed to a degree not seen in our lifetime," he
called the musicians together and asked them "to do your best and,
under no circumstances however trying, to do or say anything
which may cause friction." For his part, he stayed out of the public
eye as much as possible and never openly discussed Germany or
the Germans.

In 1915 the Boston Symphony Orchestra made its first transcontinental trip. In a special train they journeyed to San Francisco and,
at its exposition in May, played a series of thirteen concerts. When
they returned, critic Philip Hale wrote in the Boston *Herald:*

> These concerts in Boston are so remarkable, they have been so re-
> markable under the leadership of Dr. Muck, that they are now taken
> by too many as a matter of course.
>
>   For the Boston Symphony Orchestra is not merely one that con-
> tains certain accomplished virtuosos; the orchestra is a virtuoso. It
> is an instrument that, having been brought to a state of perfect
> mechanism by Dr. Muck, responds to his imaginative and poetic
> wishes. He stands there calm, undemonstrative, graceful, elegant,
> aristocratic: a man of singularly commanding and magnetic person-
> ality, even in repose. The orchestra is his speech, the expression of
> the composer's brain, heart, and soul. It is now hardly possible to
> think of this orchestra without the vision of Dr. Muck at its head as
> the interpreter of beauty and brilliance.

The war went on, and the tensions and anti-German feelings in this country were epidemic. Reporting people to the police became almost a sport, and a foreign accent was considered evidence enough. A doctor, a nationalized citizen who rode regularly from his home in Nantasket to Rowes Wharf in Boston, was reported to the coast guard for having a German accent. Thereafter, he was no longer permitted to use the ferry.

An unfortunate incident occurred at the opening concert in 1917. The American flag was not displayed as it usually had been. It was a simple oversight, remedied immediately, but in the climate of the times it was a most unfortunate one. And Major Higginson wrote sadly: "Until lately my loyalty has never been questioned." It was suggested that "The Star-Spangled Banner" be played prior to each

The orchestra on its first transcontinental tour to San Francisco.

concert as it had been at the Pops concerts all summer. He felt it to be musically inappropriate at a symphony concert. Just before a concert in Providence on October 30, 1917, the request became a demand from four subscribers who went to Charles Ellis. He and Major Higginson decided that since the musicians were already on the train it was not feasible to organize a rehearsal, and so it seemed impossible to play it that night. Muck knew nothing about the demand until the next day, when papers across the country, having picked up the story from the Providence *Journal,* announced that Muck, an enemy alien, had refused to play the national anthem. Major Higginson made a statement exonerating Muck of the false charges, requesting that if the public needed to throw stones they be thrown at him, not at the orchestra or its conductor.

Two days later Major Higginson asked Muck to play the national anthem before each concert. He replied, "What will they say to me at home?" Major Higginson said, "I do not know, but let me say this: when I am in a Catholic country and the Host is carried by, or a procession of church men comes along, I take off my hat out of consideration — not to the Host, but respect for the customs of the nation." Muck agreed to conform but at the same time expressed his desire to resign. Predictably, Major Higginson would not accept his resignation. Muck worried about being interned, but since he carried a Swiss passport and papers it was considered unlikely.

The concerts continued, and it is ironic to note a fact not known until thirty years later: the version of "The Star-Spangled Banner" Muck used initially was one by Victor Herbert. The critics considered it too "Germanic" and so another version was played. This, with the offending "Germanic" elements removed, was by the "enemy alien" concertmaster of the orchestra, Anton Witek.

After the incident in Providence, the orchestra's next trip, to New York, was marred only by gratuitous insults in the press. The ex-governor of Maryland threatened to organize a riot if the orchestra came to Baltimore. That concert was canceled.

Harassment continued. The press accused Major Higginson of hiring and harboring enemy aliens. He received many letters "begging that the concerts should go on as usual, with the same conductor and the same musicians, a few letters objected, a few were anonymous and some were very abusive and, indeed indecent." Major Higginson personally answered every letter. And he continued to have confidence in Muck, saying, "I am not at all puzzled about the right course of action in regard to the Orchestra. I think it should be maintained through the War as a valuable institution of art education." But he wrote privately to a friend who felt she could no longer go to the concerts and watch a German conductor with German musicians while her relatives fought in Europe: "I tell you, dear child, I never have had such a painful experience in this life. Certainly I tried my best to help our people and give them enjoyment and refreshment. I could go on in the same way if allowed, but at present I cannot conceive that we can play another year."

In early December 1917, Muck, at the request of the Marshal's Office in Boston, signed a document that committed him to do nothing and say nothing adverse to the United States of America. Three months later, on March 25, 1918, several marshals came to Symphony Hall during a rehearsal to arrest him. At the management's request they did at least wait until the rehearsal was over. Muck was subsequently interned at Fort Oglethorpe in Georgia. No charge was made public at the time of his arrest. However, it later became known that he went with the U.S. marshals to avoid being arrested under the Mann Act, for transporting a minor female across the state line. The twenty-year-old woman with whom he allegedly had been having an affair was a talented musician from one of Boston's socially prominent families. She had received letters from Muck that somehow had reached the attorney general's office. The "worst" of the letters included this: "I am on my way to the concert hall to entertain the crowds of dogs and swine . . . I hate to play for this rabble . . . in a short time our gracious Kaiser will smile on my request and recall me to Berlin."

This information did not appear in the papers until shortly after Major Higginson's death in 1919 — surely not a coincidence. Although he did not suffer the public indignity of it, Major Higginson no doubt understood the enormity of the harassment and was alluding to it when he wrote to his friend Charles A. Coffin: "I've turned over the charge of our Orchestra simply because of the lying dirty attacks upon it and me have used me up and given me eight weeks of real physical pain."

However, he was well enough to be able to appear at the final Friday concert on May 3, when he received an ovation from the public. On Saturday, May 4, the orchestra played in his honor his favorite Beethoven symphony, the Third. And, concluding his association with the orchestra, he read this brief address:

MY FRIENDS:

The Boston Symphony Orchestra was set up from the conviction of my youth that our country should have great and permanent orchestras. In Europe I had seen the pleasure and comfort of such orchestras, and it seemed my duty and was my aim to give our country the best music possible.

To achieve this object, it was necessary to give to the conductor the sole artistic responsibility as an essential to success, and then to require of him and of his men a high and even higher standard. To win that standard nothing has been spared and the aim never forgotten; and in this season our Orchestra has reached our high-water mark.

The concerts were offered to the whole public, but my chief wish and hope was to meet the needs, and satisfy the longings for the beautiful art of the many people leading quiet or busy lives and having little enjoyment; and furthermore, to help in the education of the students of music.

To me the concerts have been a great joy, not only because of the lovely music, but chiefly because of the refreshment and enjoyment of the multitude of people unknown to me who, leading gray lives, have needed this sunshine; and this year it is they who have written to me a mass of warm letters full of gratitude for the past and of urgent requests for the future. To these unknown friends and to all of our audiences far and wide I offer my heartiest thanks.

Thus the faith and the vision of my youth have been justified.

I had hoped to have carried on the concerts during my lifetime; but this war has brought us many troubles, and, among them, the problems of the Orchestra during this season, which have exhausted my strength and nerves. Therefore, my part in our Orchestra ceases to-night, except for the popular concerts of this year.

The conductors, the members of our Orchestra, and the office management have done their work excellently from first to last, and have deserved the warmest thanks and praise.

GENTLEMEN OF THE BOSTON SYMPHONY ORCHESTRA:

For many years we — you and I — have been good comrades — an honor and a great pleasure for me.

In these years we have worked hand and glove together, and have kept true to our rule, laid down at the outstart, of intelligent study under one conductor at a time; and we have reaped the reward of success sure to follow.

We have played in many cities of the United States, and have won great applause and, better still, have deserved it.

Each year has marked an advance in the quality of our music, and this year has seen our high point.

I like to think myself a member of our Orchestra, and have done my best to help you; and, on your side, you have served with an

Henri Rabaud conducted the orchestra for the season
1918–1919.

intelligence and devotion not to be forgotten by the audiences or by
me. I congratulate you, and thank you for our success fairly won.

My time for work is past; and now a number of excellent men and
women have taken my place. Of you I ask for them the same intelligence and devotion as in years gone by.

My best wishes go out to you.

Our Orchestra has always been heartily supported by you and by
the public throughout our country, else it could not have lived. It
must live in all its strength and beauty, and now will be carried on
by some friends who have taken it up; and for them I ask the same
support which you have given me through all these years.

The Boston Symphony Orchestra was incorporated in the spring
of 1918. Private ownership by Major Higginson was transferred to
a board of trustees composed of nine prominent citizens who assumed responsibility for it.

At the end of that season Charles Ellis also retired, to be replaced by his long-time assistant, William Brennan, and George E. Judd became assistant manager. These changes had been planned for a long time and the events of the prior months served only to hasten them. And the search for a new conductor began.

Eight or nine candidates were considered seriously for the position of conductor. Among them were Rachmaninoff, Stokowski, Toscanini, and Sir Henry Wood. It was not until September that the trustees announced their selection of Henri Rabaud. But until he was free of his duties in Paris, Pierre Monteux would lead the orchestra's first four concerts.

The weeks under Monteux's baton found the orchestra, according to critic H. T. Parker, to be "maintained, refreshed, rekindled."

Rabaud arrived in Boston in time to conduct his first concert five days after the Armistice. Born in Paris in 1873, he was the son of the professor of cello at the Paris Conservatory, where young Henri became a student of composition with Jules Massenet. He won a Prix de Rome in 1894. Rabaud became conductor of the Paris Opera Orchestra and professor of harmony at the Paris Conservatory, and later he became its director. His opera *Marouf* had been staged in New York just before his appointment in Boston.

Rabaud's stay in Boston was short. At the end of the first season, at his own request, he returned to Paris to devote his time to composition and teaching.

Chapter Four

Pierre Monteux and Serge Koussevitzky

"Do not too readily think that you have done enough, simply because you have accomplished something — There is no enough, so long as you can better the lives of your fellow beings. Your success in life depends not on talents, but on will. Surely, genius is the power of working hard, and long, and well." — Major Higginson

IN 1919 Pierre Monteux was invited to join the orchestra once again, this time as its regular conductor and music director.

Charles Munch once said that during his lifetime there were only two great conductors, Toscanini and Monteux, and the rest were still learning. Monteux is frequently referred to as the musician's, or connoisseur's, conductor. His performances were marked by a beautiful balance and blending of sound and the elegance of his impeccable musical taste. Musicians and audiences loved him. In appearance he was almost spherical, standing less than five and a half feet tall and weighing close to one hundred and ninety pounds. His hair was black, and in later years his walrus mustache was white. He was above all a gentle man, kind and jolly, but he could control the orchestra with a raised eyebrow. Having played in and been the conductor of many orchestras, Monteux was a past master in the art of running an effective rehearsal. He dealt with his musicians directly and kindly, telling them, "I don't want to follow you, so you'll have to follow me." He conducted the open rehearsals wearing a red-and-black-checked woodsman's jacket and sneakers. His conducting technique and the clarity of his beat were much admired. He had an infallible ear, and once he learned a score it was his for life. He was capable of conducting a faultless performance of a complicated work without having looked at the score for almost forty years. At his home in Hancock, Maine, he ran the Monteux School for Conductors in the summer months.

Monteux had been born in France in 1875 and studied violin at the Paris Conservatory, winning its first prize in 1896. He played viola in the Opéra Comique and Colonne Concerts and founded the Concerts Monteux in Paris, which gave prominence to contemporary works by Russian and French composers. He also conducted the orchestra for Diaghilev's Ballet Russe. These performances included the spectacular world première of Stravinsky's *Rite of Spring*, which caused a riot and forced both conductor and musicians to flee the hall. But it was not easy to ruffle Monteux.

Harry Ellis Dickson, violinist of the Boston Symphony and grateful pupil of Monteux, tells of the time when, in the middle of a

Pierre Monteux conducted from 1918 to 1924. Here he is shown much later, at a performance by the BSO of Stravinsky's *Rite of Spring* in Paris in 1956.

serious conducting class in Maine, Mrs. Monteux burst in, exclaiming that she was leaving him now and forever. There was a moment of embarrassed silence while the conductor found his way to the front of the room. "Leave the checkbook," he said and continued the class.

The period during which an orchestra receives and adjusts to its new conductor is always fraught with apprehension and uncertainty. But in 1919 the Boston Symphony faced a particularly difficult problem.

The American Federation of Musicans had been organized in 1896. One of the first unions in this country, it was the first to protect the concerns of the performed arts. From its inception Major Higginson had steadfastly refused to have anything to do with it. He believed most vehemently that if a union could dictate the number or length of rehearsals it would also become involved in other artistic decisions. When he controlled the orchestra, Major Higginson never negotiated with it as a unit and he never permitted committees or groups within the orchestra to be organized. Instead, he negotiated contracts individually with each musician. He could be so autocratic because he paid the musicians more than union wages, therefore more than musicians in other orchestras received. The Boston musicians also worked a longer season. Major Higginson always felt that the workingman should receive a larger portion of the pie, but he preferred to be the one to cut the slices.

The salaries of the Boston Symphony musicians, which had been satisfactory in 1914, were quite inadequate in 1920, after the inflation brought on by the war. Some were even earning less than in other, unionized orchestras. Under Major Higginson's benevolent patronage, no doubt the difficulties could have been "smoothed, admonished, touched up." However, Major Higginson had died in November 1919, leaving no endowment for the orchestra as he had hoped to do. The newly appointed trustees were primarily concerned with carrying on Major Higginson's policies while keeping the budget as economical as possible. The musicians' initial request for increased salaries was summarily turned down. Some musicians joined the union and used it to complain that replacements in the orchestra were being hired from abroad. Ever since the orchestra's second season, musicians had regularly been recruited in Europe by its conductors. Now, after their countries had been ravaged by war and jobs were scarce, European musicians were quite willing to work in America for less than Americans. Positions in the Boston Symphony were much sought after for the traditionally higher salaries and longer working season, and new players were hired to fill the places vacated by departing German members.

A visiting French military band left five of its members with the orchestra. One of these was the famous flutist Georges Laurent. Another was Louis Speyer, the much-admired English horn player, who never missed a rehearsal or concert in his forty-seven years with the orchestra. Georges Mager was hired to play viola until there was an opening for his preferred instrument, the trumpet. A new concertmaster was hired, the American Fredric Fradkin. His

Monteux asks for a pianissimo.

training had been with the Belgian violinist Ysaye and he had been a soloist with the New York Philharmonic under Mahler. Fradkin, whose salary was well in advance of the union scale, nevertheless joined the union in sympathy with those musicians whose salaries were not.

Tensions within the orchestra increased. On Thursday, March 4, 1920, Fradkin had a disagreement with Monteux after a concert in Cambridge. The next day the orchestra played its regularly scheduled concert in Boston. After the performance of Berlioz's *Symphonie Fantastique*, Monteux was recalled to the podium by the applause. He motioned to the orchestra to rise and share it with him. Fradkin remained seated. Disobeying the conductor at a public concert was in violation of his contract, and he was discharged by the trustees. The musicians met before the concert the next evening and voted to strike in protest of Fradkin's firing. Judge Cabot, president of the Board of Trustees, met with them, as did Monteux.

Richard Burgin, concertmaster of the orchestra from 1920 until 1962.

The audience waited in their seats, and in the musicians' tuning room there was confusion. Arthur Fiedler remembers that finally Monteux said, "All those who are going to play on this side of the room and those who are not on that side." Men ran back and forth, trying to decide what to do. Fiedler was one of thirty-six who decided to strike, although several days later he requested that he be reinstated. At eight-thirty instead of eight o'clock Monteux led the remaining fifty-six musicians in an impromptu performance of pieces requiring less than the full orchestra. As a result of the strike, thirty musicians left or were fired. After this incident, the trustees announced a major campaign for a large endowment in order that they might pay salaries competitive with union orchestras. The Boston Symphony was at the time the only major American orchestra that was nonunion; it remained so until 1942.

The concerts continued, and Pierre Monteux was asked to build up the orchestra for the second time in as many years. The thirty empty seats were initially filled by retired musicians and advanced students from the New England Conservatory. During the summer months, professional musicians were recruited to bring the orchestra back to its established size.

By the first concert of the 1920–1921 season, the orchestra had many new members, the salaries had been adjusted, and there was a new concertmaster, Richard Burgin, who remained with the orchestra until his retirement in 1962. Burgin was born in Warsaw, trained in Russia, and had been a fellow student with Jascha Heifetz of the great teacher Leopold Auer, for whom Tchaikovsky had written his violin concerto. Burgin had been a child prodigy and when he was twelve had played in New York City, where he heard the Boston Symphony play on one of its tours. He eventually came to Boston from Finland, where he had been concertmaster in Helsingfors and Christiana. A friend of composer Jan Sibelius, he had been one of the first to play his treacherously difficult violin concerto.

In the first decades of the twentieth century, the vocabulary of the language of music had expanded to include the lush romanticism of Elgar and Vaughan Williams, the early dissonances of Ravel, Satie, and Honegger, and the complicated rhythmic structures of Stravinsky's music. Even the concept of the eight-tone scale was viewed in new ways that made possible the music of Schönberg, Webern, and Berg. Monteux believed that a music director should, through his concerts, give prominence to the most varied, cosmopolitan choice of composers and to the most current expressions in the art of music. His programming was the subject of much discussion and criticism by audiences who missed the preponderance of classics interspersed with what were then called novelties. Monteux not only built up the orchestra twice, he also instilled in its audience the appreciation and taste for contemporary music. And this need was filled superbly by Koussevitzky in the next twenty-five years.

Pierre Monteux left Boston after what had become the traditional five-year term. He returned regularly as a guest conductor during Munch's tenure in the 1950s, and he was invited to conduct the Pension Fund Concert on his eightieth birthday in 1955. It was a festive occasion and is remembered by the musicians as a nostalgic highlight in their careers. The conductor chose an all-Beethoven program including the Fourth Piano Concerto and the Third Symphony, and he asked Arthur Fiedler to play the viola in the orchestra, as he had in the 1920s. Fiedler had been the conductor of the Pops since 1930 and had not even opened the case of his instrument. But he agreed, of course, and started to practice. When his children came home from school they heard him and asked their mother, "What are those strange noises coming from Daddy's study?"

On the day of the concert, flowers were hung above the stage, writing out PM and 80. In front of the stage were green wreaths and white flowers and each musician wore a white carnation. After the intermission the honoree sat smiling while Munch conducted two scores written for the occasion by two of Monteux's friends, Stravinsky and Milhaud. The dinner party after the concert included moving tributes by those whose lives he had touched. Among them was tenor Roland Hayes, who in 1923 had been the first black person to sing with a symphony orchestra in this country. Members of the orchestra played a serenade by an anonymous composer — it was, in fact, an early composition by Monteux, unearthed for the occasion by Harry Ellis Dickson and Mrs. Monteux. It was played to test the infallible memory of the old man, who of course recognized it at once, listened to it in happy embarrassment, and then announced that the composer should remain anonymous.

Monteux returned to conduct the Boston Symphony every year, including his eighty-fifth birthday celebration and the year he died, 1964, when he was almost ninety. He loved to tease. He liked to say that he began his career by playing the violin, but when he found that playing the viola was easier he switched to it. After several years of playing the viola in orchestras he discovered that conducting was much less demanding so he became a conductor. Monteux promised that when he got tired of conducting he would take on the easiest job of all — which of course was to be a music critic. He never made that final transition. He must have loved conducting too much.

Serge Koussevitzky was a legend in his lifetime and remains one long after his death. He had a flaming passion for music and he devoted his whole life to it. Koussevitzky was a conductor of high emotional fervor. A dark blood vessel pulsed on the side of his forehead during rehearsals and concerts while his aristocratic bearing and dramatic gestures were given over to the tension and force of creating a performance. That he sustained a continually growing interest in his concerts over a period of twenty-five years attests to his power of projection, the broad range of his musical interest, and his ability to sustain a level of spectacular performances. Koussevitzky was never accused of conducting a boring concert. While his interpretations of well-known works were criticized, they were also respected. And when he conducted the music he felt closest to, there was no criticism.

During the time Koussevitzky was with the Boston Symphony, he and the orchestra became a powerful force in American musical life and in the development of American music.

In those years it was expected that a conductor would be temperamental and tyrannical, but Koussevitzky's personality was extraordinary. He was a man of rages, feuds, and reconciliations, and his arrogance was absolute. After a concert one day a friend told him that he was not only the greatest conductor but the only conductor.

He replied that there probably were some fine conductors. But when asked who they were, he stared at his wife blankly, and asked, "Well, Natalya, who?" The black cape he wore was a symbol of both his elegance and his aloofness. So was the fact that he never bothered to learn idiomatic English; those who needed to, understood his wishes if not always his words.

Koussevitzky's first concern was the quality of sound. He told his orchestra, "A sound is not a beautiful noise. A sound is a *dolce* who have a beautiful round tone." A Koussevitzky rehearsal could last five hours in order to achieve the particular quality of sound he wanted.

Koussevitzky was born in Russia in 1874. He had an early interest in music and left home when he was seventeen to study in Moscow. Coming from simple circumstances he had no money for tuition, but the Moscow Philharmonic Society School offered him a scholarship and a small stipend if he would study either the trombone or double bass. Students did not often choose those instruments, and the school needed them to complete its orchestra. All his life Koussevitzky had a huge capacity for work. As a student he practiced as many as eight hours a day on the unwieldy double bass, making it capable of unusual beauty. He made such rapid progress that in his second year of study he was presented to Tchaikovsky as a virtuoso, and together they played an arrangement for piano and double bass of the *Andante Cantabile* from Tchaikovsky's First String Quartet.

After three years he left the school to join the Moscow Civic Opera Orchestra, later the Bolshoi Theatre Orchestra; at the same time he gave double bass recitals. Such was the pattern of his life for eleven years. Handsome, charming, and elegant, Koussevitzky was frequently invited to play at the elegant soirees in Moscow, at one of which he met his future wife, Natalya. This marriage changed the course and the focus of his life. With her devotion and shrewdness, Natalya also put at his disposal a vast fortune. They married in 1905 and Koussevitzky chose to break with his past.

The next four years were spent in Berlin, where the couple lived and entertained in the lavish style appropriate to the huge fortune available to them. It was there that Koussevitzky prepared for his second career. From his seat in the audience and using a score, he studied the techniques of Nikisch, Mahler, Felix Weingartner, and Felix Mottl. By watching and hearing the effects of these conductors, Koussevitzky was able to evolve a baton technique of his own. He hired a student orchestra and worked with it; then in 1908 he engaged the Berlin Philharmonic. The program was exclusively Russian music and included Rachmaninoff as the soloist in his C Minor Piano Concerto. Koussevitzky's conducting debut was a success and he scheduled more concerts. He did not, however, stop giving double bass recitals, playing to great acclaim in London, Paris, Wroclaw, Budapest, and Dresden. Under Nikisch, his idol, he played a Mozart concerto written originally for the bassoon and Bruch's *Kol Nidrei* with great success. In Dresden he performed the feat of playing Saint-Saëns's Cello Concerto on the double bass! Everywhere he went he was praised for his technique and the beauty of his tone. It was also in this period, in 1909, that Kous-

Serge Koussevitzky with his double bass in 1928. He conducted the orchestra from 1924 until 1949.

sevitzky and his wife set up l'Editions Russes, a publishing house for works by Russian composers.

Koussevitzky arranged to conduct concerts in London, Paris, and Berlin, where he received congratulations from Nikisch: "I am astonished. You have been conducting only for such a short time and can do all this? You are a born conductor."

The Koussevitzkys returned to Moscow, where in 1911 he organized an orchestra to give concerts at popular prices. Salaries were generous and there was a pension fund. Any profits were to go to the musicians; any deficit was guaranteed by the conductor. This was the first permanent Russian orchestra formed for the exclusive task of playing orchestral concerts. Its schedule was quite complicated. The season consisted of eight weekly programs that alternated between Moscow and St. Petersburg, to which the orchestra traveled by special train. The orchestra played pops concerts on Sundays, under guest conductors, as well as a series of chamber music recitals. Choruses were organized in both Moscow and St. Petersburg to assist in the presentation of choral works. During these concerts all Beethoven's symphonies were played and new Russian works and those by Debussy, Bruckner, and Mahler were introduced. Debussy visited Koussevitzky in Moscow and said he had never heard so many of his works at one time. He also commented on Koussevitzky's need and will to serve music. Stravinsky's *Petrouchka*, which had recently been issued by l'Editions Russes, received its first concert performances at this time.

Koussevitzky devised the incredible plan of chartering a huge pleasure boat and, with the orchestra members, their wives, children, and his own entourage, sailing down the Volga River. Much of the river is frozen for almost half the year, and so spring comes late to the Volga. In some places, where it is swollen with melting snow and ice, the river is a mile wide. In the summer months it carried a variety of craft, from the large pleasure boats and freighters to huge, crude log rafts that carried whole nomadic villages south after the winter. During May nineteen concerts were scheduled going downstream, and several stops were made on the return trip for additional concerts. Some of the towns along the way had been built by the Tartars more than a thousand years before. Some villages were nomadic, with primitive people who lived in tents and worshiped Buddha. At Kostroma, a town of forty-five thousand people where the first Romanov had been crowned more than three hundred years before, the musicians found a statue to Glinka, considered the father of modern Russian music. In these towns and primitive villages, many of which had never heard an orchestra before, Koussevitzky with all his fire and passion conducted works of Beethoven, Tchaikovsky, Rachmaninoff, and Scriabin, who was the soloist in his own piano concerto. Along the way Koussevitzky listened to and encouraged local musicians. He made it possible for those who were particularly gifted to study in Moscow. Three summer expeditions were made in 1910, 1912, and 1914. At one small town on the third trip the boat was greeted by a fanfare from a local "band Koussevitsky" inspired by a previous visit!

In 1914 war broke out, followed in 1917 by the Russian Revolution. Koussevitzky continued to organize and conduct concerts during this extended period of upheaval. Living and working conditions in Moscow were terrible and even the privileged suffered. It was during this time that Koussevitzky conducted opera for the first time, Tchaikovsky's *Queen of Spades* at the Bolshoi Theatre. This performance was remembered as exciting by a young cellist in the orchestra, Gregor Piatigorsky. After the Revolution, orchestras in Moscow became nationalized; and even though he was considered one of Russia's great conductors, Koussevitzky was no longer permitted to manage and arrange concerts as he wished. Also, and more important, the large fortune that sustained him was confiscated. In the spring of 1920 the Koussevitzkys obtained permission to leave the country and went to live in Paris.

The family holdings had not been limited to Russia, and in Paris they pursued life in much the same style as they had in Moscow. In 1921 Koussevitzky organized a series of four concerts, to be known as the Concerts Koussevitzky. These concerts, held in the beautiful Opéra, were a spectacular success and turned out to be the most fashionable affair in Paris. Koussevitzky became the grand seigneur of music in Paris. Once again his own manager, he chose the finest musicians and rehearsed them as much as he wanted. The highlights of these concerts were the performances of contemporary works by Ravel, Stravinsky, Prokofiev, Honegger, and Milhaud. It was Koussevitzky who suggested to Ravel that he make the orchestral transcription of Moussorgsky's *Pictures at an Exhibition,* which remained Koussevitzky's exclusive property for many years. Koussevitzky the publisher always worked closely with Koussevitzky the conductor.

In 1923 it was announced that Koussevitzky had been offered and had accepted the position of conductor of the Boston Symphony Orchestra, beginning the following year. This appointment firmly established Koussevitzky as a respected professional conductor. That season the Concerts Koussevitzky were particularly successful, with news of his appointment stimulating the interest of both the audience and the press.

To follow in the steps of his idol Nikisch and become conductor of the Boston Symphony was a hope Koussevitzky had long cherished, and in September 1924 he and his wife left Paris for Boston.

Even before he arrived the new conductor made himself felt. Through a supportive management he let it be known that the major work or symphony would come at the end of the program rather than at the beginning, that there was to be no applause between movements of a work, that soloists would be called "assisting artists" and would be used only where they contributed to the overall symphonic content of the programs. Clearly these were to be Koussevitzky's performances.

On the afternoon of October 10, 1924, the new music director stepped on stage promptly at two-thirty to a standing ovation. Always the suave diplomat, he acknowledged the applause of his orchestra before turning to the audience. The program was typical of the pattern he was to follow: a brief work of Vivaldi, one of the then-neglected eighteenth-century composers; a showpiece, Berlioz's *Roman Carnival* Overture; Brahms's Haydn Variations; Honegger's *Pacific 231;* ending with an impassioned performance of Scriabin's *Poem of Ecstasy.*

The effect of the concert was electric. Critic Philip Hale wrote: "Mr. Koussevitzky has a commanding figure and that indefinable quality known as magnetism which works its spell on orchestra and audience . . . He at once inspires confidence, expectation, curiosity . . ." And Olin Downes, who had come from New York for the occasion, wrote: "His authority is so complete that it is sensed before it is demonstrated . . . He is a musician who feels deeply his

Four composers whose music played an important role in the programs of the orchestra: the young Brahms *(The Bettmann Archive, Inc.)*, Gustav Mahler, Béla Bartók *(The Bettmann Archive, Inc.)*, Serge Prokofiev *(The Bettmann Archive, Inc.)*.

mission, who interprets with flaming temperament and communicative power.'' Immediately Koussevitzky became the grand seigneur, and for twenty-five years music in Boston revolved around his personality.

The indefinable quality of magnetism did indeed work its spell on audiences. It also elicited from his musicians performances that left each one emotionally spent and wringing wet after every concert. This projection was Koussevitzky's gift, one that is shared by only the greatest conductors.

Even though he received from Monteux a highly trained and disciplined orchestra, it took Koussevitzky nearly four years to build and shape it as he wanted. They were difficult years for several reasons.

As a student Koussevitzky had devoted his energies to the task of becoming a virtuoso performer on the double bass. The basic groundwork and knowledge required to be a conductor — in harmony, music theory, composition, and the ready ability to comprehend and interpret music as it appears on a large orchestral score — had all been neglected in his studies. He was not a highly educated musician with the broad conducting experience of Muck or Monteux. He had, of course, conducted many concerts before he came to Boston, but they were usually four or eight performances in a season arranged and paid for by himself. He had never been faced with the task of preparing twenty-four different programs in a season, conducting more than one hundred concerts within thirty weeks, and by doing so please a knowledgeable audience. The combination of his natural talent, his imperious will, and his passion to serve music made it possible for him, at the age of fifty, to learn at rehearsals and in public concerts what he should have learned as a student thirty years before.

Koussevitzky's rehearsals were strenuous ordeals. He rehearsed music at the same energy level as that of a performance. He held his musicians in high regard, considering each one a great artist. But his treatment of them in rehearsal was abusive, sadistic, and frequently humiliating. The quality of sound was the only thing that mattered to Koussevitzky, and everything and everyone was subservient to it. At the slightest lack of concentration or laxity on the part of the players, he would fly into a rage and make each player stand up and play the section alone. It was not unusual for him to throw the score or leave the hall in a towering rage. Harold C. Schonberg, music critic of the *New York Times,* tells the story of the Boston musician who was gravely ill. Koussevitzky went to see him. With the impunity of approaching death, the musician told Koussevitzky what a bully, a tyrant, and what an arrogant and generally terrible man he was, then lay back prepared to die happy. But Koussevitzky was bewildered. "You should know that I am your father. You are my children." The musician did actually recover and in some embarrassment returned to the orchestra. Koussevitzky never forgave him.

Koussevitzky did feel that he was the father and the musicians his children, and when they did not please him he would say, "You are bad *Kinder,* but you are my *Kinder.*" He worried about their health, insisting they wear hats in winter and not drink cold water too soon after performances. But he continued his rages and abusiveness. The musicians were in a difficult position. Many were from abroad, some hardly spoke English, and their security with the orchestra was their life. Since the Boston Symphony was the only major nonunion orchestra, it was virtually impossible to get a job elsewhere, and the players lived in fear of being summarily fired during a Koussevitzky rage. Curiously, from this negative paternalism grew one of Koussevitzky's greatest legacies. Out of their will to survive came the ability of the musicians to listen to one another during performances, to set up signals with each other for the times when Koussevitzky's indications were wrong, incoherent, or both. Consequently the orchestra played with the finesse of a great chamber music group. Koussevitzky's conducting improved over the years, but the esprit de corps remained and is still present today.

Even during those early difficult years, when Koussevitzky was still learning his profession and the musicians were learning how to get along with him, the concerts had the spectacular success that Koussevitzky maintained until his retirement. The intervening years were ones of glorious music-making and included festivals of compositions by Beethoven, Brahms, and Sibelius; Bach's great choral works were performed, accompanied by the Harvard and Radcliffe choruses.

But it was Koussevitzky, egocentric and glamorous, who established precedents and set standards of excellence in his adopted country. With his extraordinary intuition Koussevitzky sought out, sometimes commissioned, but, above all, with his orchestra performed a continuing flow of contemporary music from Russia, western Europe, and the United States. Sometimes composers came as soloists or as conductors of their works, and they were always grateful to the man who gave them the opportunity to be heard. A list of world premières given by Koussevitzky and the Boston Symphony includes virtually every composer of stature of the times, a record not duplicated either before or since.

At the turn of the century a music critic had said that the entire number of American composers could be lodged quite comfortably in the double room of a country inn. Koussevitzky changed that. "It is the duty of American orchestras to give due representation to the work of American composers. They must work, and the orchestras must play their music," he said. The list of works by composers of the United States that he brought to the public is six pages long. The performance of these works recognized and encouraged native talent in a way that was valuable and perhaps his greatest legacy.

Another was the Berkshire Music Festival, which he took over in 1936. There he created a music school in 1940 that has produced highly trained musicians and from his own conducting classes conductors of stature, among them his favorite pupil, Leonard Bernstein, who now wears the legendary black cape. Seiji Ozawa, another student of the Berkshire Music Center who worked not with Koussevitzky but with his successor, Charles Munch, became the music director of the Boston Symphony in 1973.

Koussevitzky retired in 1949 and died in Boston two years later. Expressions of this man's special genius remain in abundance. Even today, people speak of him with awe. And when musicians long since retired from the orchestra hear his voice on tape saying crisply, "Gentlemen, it is very not together," cold shivers still run down their spines.

Chapter Five

Charles Munch to Seiji Ozawa

"I have never cared about money for its own sake, have had the good luck to get considerable, and have spent of it as well as I could. It isn't bread and butter we want half as much as it is pleasant, friendly relations with our fellow creatures."
— Major Higginson

WHEN KOUSSEVITZKY RETIRED, he suggested that Charles Munch succeed him as conductor. No two men could have had more different personalities, and their approaches to music were correspondingly different. Where Koussevitzky's concern was the *sound* of the orchestra, Munch was concerned with the *phrasing* of the music. A man of elegance and sophisticated tastes, he was also a private man, modest and gentle. Constant learning and study were in his view the essence of the conductor's life. Munch was forty-two when he chose to become a conductor, and he pursued his profession with the profound humility of a man following a sacred calling.

Long after he had retired from the Boston Symphony, Charles Munch was visiting and conducting in Japan. Seiji Ozawa, his former pupil, congratulated him: "And now your life is easy, you only conduct your favorite music, no more work."

"Ah, but you are wrong," said Munch. "Every day I must study these scores for many hours. Even now I learn something new." These were works he had conducted literally hundreds of times. During the course of his career, he periodically returned quietly to the classroom to learn more. Sometimes he listened to the competi-

Three conductors together: Pierre Monteux, Serge Koussevitzky, and Charles Munch, who became music director in 1949.

tions at the conservatories. After hearing fifteen clarinetists in succession play a difficult solo, he was able to refresh his understanding of what that instrument's possibilities were.

Once, when he was already a respected conductor and Toscanini came to Paris to conduct, Munch arranged to play in Toscanini's orchestra so that he might have the opportunity to watch and learn from the maestro at first hand.

Charles Munch grew up in an intensely musical and scholarly atmosphere. He was born in Strasbourg, Alsace, in 1891. Both his father and uncle were gifted organists. His uncle had been the first teacher of Albert Schweitzer, who was the organist at a neighboring church. Young Charles sang in his father's choir and frequently replaced him as organist. The Munch household was the meeting place for many musicians and became the scene of lively discussions that centered on music, its performance, and its interpretation. Strasbourg was one of the music centers of Europe, and during his youth Munch attended concerts conducted by von Bülow, Nikisch, Richard Strauss, Weingartner, Mahler, and Bruno Walter. Young Charles was a student at the Strasbourg Conservatory, where he received a thorough musical training. His instrument was the violin. After his graduation, he went to Paris to pursue his study of the violin with Lucien Capet.

Alsace has spent part of its history under French rule and part under German. During the First World War it belonged to the German Empire. Due to the accident of boundary, Albert Schweitzer was interned as an enemy alien and Charles Munch was forced to fight for Germany. After the war Munch became assistant concertmaster of the Strasbourg Orchestra and was also professor of violin at the conservatory. From there he went to Leipzig and for eight years was the concertmaster of the Gewandhaus Orchestra, conducted by Felix Weingartner, who became a close friend. Each Sunday Munch played in the chamber orchestra that accompanied the Bach cantatas that were sung in the Thomaskirche, where Bach

Charles Munch conducts a quiet passage.

Munch in a moment of ecstasy *(Gilbert E. Friedberg)*.

had himself been cantor. Munch conducted for the first time at Thomaskirche, filling in for the indisposed cantor. A short time later, after his second conducting experience, he laid aside his violin for good.

It was 1932, and with the radical changes in the political scene, Munch went to live in Paris. There in November he engaged the internationally acclaimed Straram Orchestra. His debut was a success, and he promptly received invitations to conduct other orchestras that same season. The following year he formed an orchestra of his own and with predictable modesty called it the Paris Philharmonic. He soon became identified with exciting performances of contemporary music. Munch played music that fascinated him. He also played what he thought should be heard: complete works by little-known as well as known composers, new works by living composers, among them Honegger, Roussel, Martinů, and Poulenc. The orchestra played at the Paris meeting of the International Society for Contemporary Music. Munch was also in great demand as a guest conductor and visited London, Prague, Budapest, and Vienna in that capacity.

In 1937 Munch was invited to become conductor of the Paris Conservatory Orchestra, France's most prestigious symphony. There his programs included a broader range of music, and he conducted its concerts each Sunday until 1945. The outbreak of World War II found Munch in Lisbon, on his way to guest-conduct in America. He returned immediately to Paris and his orchestra. Later he recalled:

> During the four terrible years of German occupation my role was to help saddened souls escape to happier worlds. I worked at it with an ardor that was multiplied a thousand fold by the pain of seeing my country gagged, enchained and murdered.

He also helped to support the Resistance financially. His country house was a crucial part of the escape network for prisoners of war and the Allied plane crews who had been forced down over occupied territory.

Immediately following the war Munch did come to America and was a guest conductor in Boston as well as in other major cities. In 1949 he returned to tour the United States with the French National Radio Orchestra. Later that year he became conductor of the Boston Symphony.

In some sense history was repeating itself. When Nikisch took over the orchestra after Gericke's years of drilling and training, he had said, "All I have to do is poetize." The orchestra that Munch took over was a finely tuned and disciplined instrument. A concert for Koussevitzky had been the impassioned recreation of what had preceded in arduous rehearsal. A concert for Munch was a creative explosion, the culmination at that moment of his private study and intuition. It was not necessarily the result of prior rehearsals, which he often cut short of the allotted time. With the gift of Koussevitzky's superb instrument, Munch was able to do what he did best: interpret. "The public will not strain itself to hang a dream on every note. It is for us to facilitate their task."

It was a different dream each time; no two performances of the same work were alike. Roger Voisin, first trumpet under Munch, remembers going on a tour that he had thought might be a bit boring, for one of the works scheduled each night was the "Love Scene" from Berlioz's *Romeo et Juliette*. This section is scored for strings only, so Voisin, a restless man, was required to sit perfectly still during its performance. However, he found that each day he looked forward to seeing what magic Munch would weave with the music. Each night it was extraordinarily evocative and beautiful — and always different.

Munch's specialty was the performance of the brilliant, glittering French repertoire: the music of Debussy, Berlioz, Ravel, and Poulenc. He wrote once: "Some [conductors] have built their entire careers on a dozen scores — and not from laziness but humble prudence." In his later years Munch's programs were almost exclusively French. When Nikisch left Boston in 1893, a critic noted, "When at his best, he was simply glorious." The same can be said of Munch.

"Le Beau Charles," as he was known in France, was an exciting and graceful conductor to watch. He held the baton lightly in a simple extension of his arm, which made large, strong sweeping gestures. His left hand, gracefully describing the nuances, often vibrated close to his heart, asking for more.

Munch's thirteen-year tenure with the Boston Symphony was highlighted by three international tours. The first was made in 1952 at the invitation of the Congress for Cultural Freedom. Munch and guest conductor Pierre Monteux gave concerts in eleven cities in Europe, including London, Berlin, and Amsterdam. The tour also included a performance in Frankfurt, for those American troops still in Germany, and an opportunity for Munch to conduct his orchestra in Strasbourg, the town of his birth and childhood. Another highlight of the tour was a concert in Paris in which Monteux conducted *Le Sacre du Printemps* in the same theater in which he had conducted its première forty years before. Stravinsky was in the audience, jubilant.

The second European tour was more extensive. The Boston Symphony Orchestra was the first Western orchestra to be heard in the Soviet Union. It played two concerts in Leningrad and three in Moscow. These concerts were accompanied by festive receptions and a formal state dinner after the last concert in Moscow. Many toasts and speeches of gratitude were made. Among those who

Members of the orchestra with their wives in
Moscow's Red Square.

spoke were Soviet composers Kabalevsky, Shostakovich, and
Khachaturian; violinists David Oistrakh and Leonard Kogan; cellist
Mstislav Rostropovich; and conductor Kyril Kondrashin. The ova-
tions and recognition came not only from the public and official
sources. The musicians were touched and delighted to be greeted
at the stage door after their concerts by their counterparts in the
Moscow and Leningrad orchestras, bringing them roses. In Paris
concerts were played in memory of Serge Koussevitzky and composer Georges Enesco. At Chartres Cathedral, Munch and the orchestra played a memorable and moving concert beneath its rose
window. The program included Honegger's *Sinfonie Liturgique* and
the Third Symphony of Beethoven.

The orchestra performed for the first time in Vienna, Prague,
Dublin, and at the Edinburgh Festival in Scotland. The symphony,

which under Koussevitzky had been the greatest champion of Sibelius's music, also made a pilgrimage to Helsinki and played in his honor. The aging composer was by then, however, a recluse and unable to attend the concert. He was well enough to receive a visit from Koussevitzky's widow, who was with the orchestra at the time.

Four years later, in 1960, the Boston Symphony was invited to the Far East, where, in Japan, Munch and his orchestra were greeted with affection and excitement. He found the Japanese audiences to be among the most appreciative in the world. Tickets were sold out long before the concerts and were so in demand that people even shared them, one person using it for the first half and a second after the intermission.

The orchestra played twenty-two concerts in Japan. The Japanese *Times* wrote:

> Beyond all its virtuoso capabilities, the Boston Symphony Orchestra provides one of those all-too-rare exquisite, civilized pleasures of music making on the highest spheres. In every respect, it is the most aristocratic, musically mature and technically distinguished of American symphonic ensembles.

This was the most extended of its tours, as the symphony also played in Taiwan, the Philippines, Australia, and New Zealand before returning to Boston and its regular schedule.

In the 1950s the Boston Symphony was in its eighth decade, an institution truly "musically mature and technically distinguished." It was the product of all its musicians and all its conductors. That it was chosen to represent the United States as its cultural ambassador following the war was a tribute not only to the orchestra's current excellence. It was also a tribute to the tradition of its vital role in the musical history and life of its country, a tradition that had its roots in Major Higginson's original plan and statement of 1881. He would have been gratified.

On Munch's retirement in 1962 Erich Leinsdorf came to Boston. At the age of fifty he was a world-famous conductor with a substantial, successful career already to his credit.

Leinsdorf was born in Vienna in 1912 and showed his gift for music early. He studied at the Vienna University and at the State

Erich Leinsdorf became music director in 1962. Here, he sits in front of the portrait of Major Higginson. Henry Cabot, president of the Board of Trustees, reads an announcement.

Academy of Music. His first instrument was the piano, his second the cello. In 1933, when he graduated, the political situation requiring "racial Aryan purity" made it impossible for him to follow the usual course of young conductors, who learned their profession as assistants to those in state or municipal posts. Instead, Leinsdorf became the accompanist for a famous voice coach, which led quickly to his accompanying opera productions under Bruno Walter at the Salzburg Festival. He also became Toscanini's assistant in Salzburg and in the Opera House in Vienna. This association had a great effect on his musical life. On Toscanini's recommendation, Leinsdorf was hired by the Metropolitan Opera in New York to assist Artur Bodanzky. Leinsdorf made his debut in January 1938, conducting *Die Walküre* by Wagner. He was twenty-five years old. Bodanzky died in 1939, and Leinsdorf took over the conducting of the German repertoire. He stayed at the Met until 1943, with visits to the San Francisco Opera Company during that time as well as later. Having become an American citizen in 1941, he served briefly in the U.S. Army before taking up the position of conductor of the Cleveland Orchestra in 1943. In so doing, he became the youngest conductor of a major American orchestra. After his stay in Cleveland, Leinsdorf returned to the Met for one season, following which he spent nine years as conductor of the Rochester Philharmonic. For one season he was the director of the New York City Opera and, prior to the Boston appointment, he again conducted at the Metropolitan Opera from 1957 to 1962.

Erich Leinsdorf has enormous energy and a great capacity for work. He is not a conductor who relies on the inspiration of the moment. His approach is intellectual, methodical, and thorough. His performances, whether of opera or symphonic music, are marked by his serious concern for musical authenticity. He is a musician of remarkably broad range and conducts with equal effect works by composers as different as Verdi, Prokofiev, and Mozart. Some of his performances of the large works by the German symphonists Brahms, Bruckner, and Mahler have been outstanding. Leinsdorf is an intellectual man, knowledgeable on many subjects, articulate, and often outspoken. He is also a man of many ideas, and his tenure in Boston was marked by innovation and change. After two years there were many new faces in the orchestra; some players had been asked to retire, others had wished to. Among the latter was concertmaster Richard Burgin. The new concertmaster came from within the orchestra itself: Joseph Silverstein, who had joined the Boston Symphony in 1955. He has appeared regularly as a soloist with the orchestra and is also a member of the Boston Symphony Chamber Players. This group of twelve musicians from the orchestra was one of Leinsdorf's ideas and was formed at his suggestion in 1964. Since then the Chamber Players have toured the United States, Europe, Russia, and South America to great acclaim. One of their recordings has won a Grammy Award. It was also Leinsdorf who initiated concert performances of operas, and he organized and trained the Tanglewood Chorus to assist in such performances as well as in the large choral works of Bach, Haydn, Handel, and Mozart. He built up the Berkshire Music Center and the Tanglewood Concert Series to an exciting level of excellence. And his programming was a masterpiece of long-range planning, intelligent and broad in its scope.

It fell to Erich Leinsdorf to announce to the stunned orchestra and audience of the Friday afternoon concert of November 22, 1963, that

Erich Leinsdorf in a quiet moment.

The original Boston Symphony Chamber Players: standing from left to right, George Moleux (bass); Everett Firth (timpani); Roger Voisin (trumpet); William Gibson (trombone); James Stagliano (horn). Seated from left to right: Joseph Silverstein (violin); Burton Fine (viola); Jules Eskin (cello); Doriot Anthony Dwyer (flute); Ralph Gomberg (oboe); Gino Cioffi (clarinet); Sherman Walt (bassoon).

President John F. Kennedy had been assassinated. He then led the orchestra in the slow movement of Beethoven's Third Symphony. The audience stood while the musicians played, weeping. Later the orchestra participated in a more formal tribute: the performance of Mozart's *Requiem* at a High Mass in the Cathedral of the Holy Cross in Boston led by Cardinal Cushing with members of the late President's family present.

Koussevitzky's reign had required everyone to be subservient to his performance of music; that included trustees, management, composers, musicians, and the audience. Munch's tenure was one of recovery. In the complex world of the 1960s, the unquestioned autocracy of a conductor was no longer acceptable to anyone. Self-effacement on the part of management and polite aloofness of trustees were no longer appropriate to the responsibilities at hand. Leinsdorf, impatient and demanding, strove to define and establish what the job of music director and conductor should be for a twentieth-century orchestra. It was in this attempt to establish values and standards and to define responsibilities that friction and ultimate disagreement occurred.

Leinsdorf resigned in 1969. He has gone on to reap the benefits of being a permanent guest conductor, a most successful career that has taken him around the world several times.

Immediately following Leinsdorf's departure, the orchestra was conducted by its new music director, William Steinberg. His career has been one noted not only for his conducting but also for his building of orchestras. His tenure in Boston was short; he retired in 1972 because of poor health, which had plagued him throughout his appointment.

Steinberg was born in 1899 in Cologne and graduated from its

The Boston Symphony Chamber Players in the 1970s: from bottom step, Joseph Silverstein (violin); Jules Eskin (cello); Doriot Anthony Dwyer (flute); Charles Kavaloski (horn); Sherman Walt (bassoon); Everett Firth (timpani); Harold Wright (clarinet); Ralph Gomberg (oboe); Armando Ghitalla (trumpet); Henri Portnoi (bass); Burton Fine (viola); William Gibson (trombone).

conservatory, where, in addition to conducting, he had also studied piano and violin. He became assistant to Otto Klemperer at the Cologne Opera. Later he became opera director at Prague for two years before going to Frankfurt as music director of its opera. There he conducted first performances of important contemporary works, including Berg's *Wozzeck* and Weill's *Mahagonny*. Dismissed from his official post by the Nazis, Steinberg founded the Jewish Culture League in Frankfurt and conducted opera and concerts for Jewish audiences. He finally left Germany in 1936 to found, with cellist Bronislav Huberman, the Palestine Orchestra, now known as the Israel Philharmonic. Its inaugural concert was conducted by Toscanini, who invited Steinberg to come to the United States to assist in the formation and building of the NBC Symphony. He then conducted the Buffalo Philharmonic for seven

William Steinberg took over from Leinsdorf in 1969 and remained music director until 1972, when he retired because of ill health.

Michael Tilson Thomas, who produced the Spectrum
Series of contemporary programs, often stood in for
Steinberg *(Gilbert E. Friedberg)*.

years, until he became music director of the Pittsburgh Symphony
in 1952. Under his direction it became one of America's foremost
orchestras.

Steinberg was one of the first conductors to divide his time between two orchestras, a practice now prevalent. Between 1958 and
1960 he traveled between Pittsburgh and London, where he was
music director of the London Philharmonic. In 1964 he was the
principal guest conductor of the New York Philharmonic while still
music director of the Pittsburgh orchestra. During his Boston tenure he divided his time equally between its orchestra and Pittsburgh's.

At an early rehearsal in Boston, he told the orchestra how, when
he had first come to this country, he had heard the orchestra play in

Seiji Ozawa became music director of the orchestra in 1972.

New York under Koussevitzky. The concert had been a revelation
to the young conductor as he realized how beautifully the musicians played together. It was his hope that he could make the orchestra sound like that again. It was sad that he came to Boston at
a time when he was beset by failing energy and illness. Although
his problems caused him to miss concerts frequently, it did not
exclude some extraordinarily beautiful performances, particularly of
works by Bruckner and Mahler. His illness was the vehicle for the
gifted young Michael Tilson Thomas to begin his own career at the
very top. A month after his appointment as assistant conductor in
1969, he substituted for Steinberg in the middle of a concert and
received immediate acclaim. He has since left the orchestra to become music director at Buffalo.

Seiji Ozawa, the thirteenth music director of the Boston Symphony Orchestra, is a man who enjoys. Conducting gives him profound pleasure, and he understands instinctively that musicians
play their best only when they too enjoy. In his own way and with
few words, Ozawa has established an atmosphere in Symphony
Hall that reflects his own enthusiasm and delight in being there.
The musicians now look forward to their concerts with a height-
ened sense of anticipation. In the audience and on stage there is
a feeling of excitement before each concert.

Ozawa is a totally graceful conductor. The movement of his body
anticipates the music, never intruding on it or becoming irritating.
When he first conducted the orchestra his body was his language,
for he spoke virtually no English. The musicians respect his musical knowledge. They find him comfortable to play with and per-
ceive his gestures and physical movements as extraordinarily
informative.

It is appropriate that he was chosen to come to Boston. Two of
his three greatest influences were Charles Munch and Leonard
Bernstein and he was a student at Tanglewood. In choosing a man
in his thirties, the trustees returned to Major Higginson's philosophy of preferring the enthusiasm of a new career to the experience
of a more established one. And Ozawa joins Max Fiedler, Koussevitzky, and Munch in that his training and experience had been
primarily as a conductor of orchestral concerts.

His career is particularly interesting because he is enormously gifted. But it is also interesting because he is part of the post–World War II generation of conductors who had very different resources and opportunities available to them from those who came before.

Ozawa has a Christian mother and a Buddhist father; consequently he studied both Western and Oriental music as a child. He was born in 1935 in Manchuria but spent much of his childhood in Japan, where he went to music school in Tokyo. His instrument was the piano until a rugby injury to a finger turned him to composition and conducting. Professor Saito at the Toho Music School remains a powerful influence on his life. It was from him that young Seiji learned the essential value of systematic and thorough preparation before the first rehearsal. And he also learned much about the scope of different musical traditions. Seiji made such swift progress that he was invited to conduct several Japanese orchestras. He received various honors in 1959, including the outstanding talent of the year award from the Japanese National Radio. Professor Saito urged young Seiji to expand his horizons and go to Europe to study. Only a few months later, at the International Competition of Orchestra Conductors at Besançon, France, he won first prize. Charles Munch, then conductor of the Boston Symphony, was present. He invented Seiji to come to America and study at the Berkshire Music Center the following summer. This he did, and he received the Koussevitzky Memorial Scholarship as the outstanding young conductor at the center. During that summer he conducted the Boston Symphony. Harold Schonberg wrote in the *New York Times:* "Here is a name to remember — Seiji Ozawa. Yesterday afternoon he conducted the Boston Symphony Orchestra and left no doubt that he is a major talent. He has a good deal of temperament, a propulsive rhythm and thorough command over his forces. Mr. Ozawa is a young man who will go far."

Soon after these prophetic words, and having won a scholarship to study with Herbert von Karajan, Ozawa left for West Berlin. There Leonard Bernstein saw him conduct and invited him to go with the New York Philharmonic on its tour of Japan in 1961. Returning to New York, Seiji became one of his assistant conductors. In that same season he conducted the San Francisco Orchestra as its guest conductor. As a last-minute replacement for a sick conductor at Chicago's Ravinia Festival, Ozawa received acclaim and a five-year contract to be its music director. Ozawa made his debut with the Toronto Symphony during the 1963–1964 season and the following season was appointed its music director. He held this position until the end of the 1968–1969 season, when he decided to devote his time to study and to guest conducting. Gaining experience as guest conductor of orchestras in this country and Europe, Ozawa also conducted opera for the first time in 1969 at the Salzburg Festival. In 1970 he became the music director of the San Francisco Orchestra and with it toured Europe and the Soviet Union.

The music industry is such that contracts for soloists and conductors have to be drawn up several years in advance. When a conductor suddenly resigns or has to withdraw because of illness, as Steinberg did, the trustees often have a problem, not in knowing who they want to be conductor, but in matching their wish with his availability. So for three years after Steinberg retired, Ozawa divided his time between the Boston and San Francisco orchestras. In addition to those duties, in 1973 he conducted six performances of Tchaikovsky's *Eugene Onegin* at London's Covent Garden Opera House. The following year he also conducted the European tour of the New Japan Philharmonic.

Seiji Ozawa's breathtaking ascent, which began so near the pinnacle, clearly indicates different opportunities and training from those who preceded him as conductors in Boston. Most of those conductors spent some time early in their careers playing an instrument in an orchestra, as Nikisch, Koussevitzky, and Monteux all did. Ozawa did not. Excepting those who could afford to hire and form their own orchestras, like Koussevitzky and Munch, virtually all learned their profession and the large repertory it requires in the European tradition of apprenticeship. Leinsdorf worked in this way with Bruno Walter and Toscanini. When Munch was a student he waited for the great conductors of Europe to visit Strasbourg. If they were lucky he and his fellow students heard at intervals music that they perhaps had never heard before. When Ozawa was a student in the 1950s, he was able to go to the record store and buy several different performances of an ever-increasing repertory of recorded classical music.

Erich Leinsdorf is fond of saying that musical standards are now set at the nearest record store. The implications of that for the younger generation of conductors is enormous. Of course nothing substitutes for a thorough, basic education in music. But having that as well as the opportunity to hear how other and great conductors have interpreted a score has placed in the hands of aspiring conductors a priceless body of knowledge not previously available. Also, with this vast resource, the process of introduction to the large and continually growing repertory has been telescoped. Another aspect of modern technology has diffused the national traditions of training for conductors. With the possibilities made available by jet travel, student conductors are able to seek out and take advantage of training in various countries, as Seiji Ozawa did: first in Japan, then in France, on to America, back to Europe — this time to Germany — back to Japan, and back to America. His contemporaries have followed similar patterns.

Just before the Second World War, the United States found itself the grateful host to a number of conductors from Europe who were fleeing the oppressions of Nazi Germany and Fascist Italy. This long list includes Toscanini, Bruno Walter, Otto Klemperer, Erich Leinsdorf, and William Steinberg. Others, like Fritz Reiner, were caught here during guest-conducting trips at the outbreak of the war and stayed. These men, nearly all trained in either Austria or Germany, contributed an immeasurable amount to musical development and traditions in America. They became conductors of the orchestras in the big cities of this country, building them up to the equivalent of those they left in Europe. After the war the borders of Russia and eastern Europe were closed, and the flow of conductors from that part of the world came abruptly to a halt. By the 1960s, and certainly by the early 1970s, many of the conductors who had come over in the 1930s had either died or retired. These two unrelated, concurrent situations created a sudden dearth of conductors in this country. This happened at a time when many orchestras were extending their seasons and adding summer festivals in order to provide full-year contracts for their musicians.

It was these events that marked the beginning of a new era of divided leadership of orchestras. Instead of each orchestra having two leaders, one conductor now frequently has two orchestras.

Seiji Ozawa in rehearsal at Tanglewood.

With one repertory a conductor is able to schedule those works with both orchestras and in addition be able to make guest-conducting appearances. In this way the concerts of longer seasons and increasing summer festivals can be filled. This shift gave young conductors like Seiji Ozawa the extraordinarily valuable opportunity to conduct a number and variety of orchestras, including the great ones, early in their careers. Certainly not all the novices had the talent or fortitude to survive the immediate exposure, the pressures, or the continual traveling that was required.

For their entire two-hundred-year history, orchestral concerts were dominated until the end of the Second World War by conductors of the Austrian-German tradition. No one tradition now dominates. Lorin Maazel, James Levine, and Michael Tilson Thomas are Americans. Claudio Abbado is Italian. Colin Davis, the Boston Symphony's principal guest conductor, is English. Zubin Mehta is from India. Seiji Ozawa is from Japan. But Mehta's concerts do not have an Indian quality. Nor do Ozawa's have a Japanese sound. These men and their contemporaries are not identifiable in performance as coming from a specific musical tradition or nation.

Today's conductors are creative artists in the language of the silent gesture. They have become traveling virtuoso performers, and are looked upon by their musicians as essential, authoritative musical information centers. They look upon music much as they look upon themselves: national in origin, international in spirit, with a vital life of its own. Ozawa professes not to feel more comfortable in one tradition or period of music than in another. He says it is like cooking: "With French food you use one set of ingredients, with German another. The same is true in the preparation of music."

Clearly conductors have moved on to a different place in their evolution. So have musicians. In the early days of orchestras in this country, musicians were grateful to receive a nominal wage. Now, just one hundred years later, being a musician in an orchestra means to have a respected, full-time profession. With its opportunities for recordings, solo performances, chamber concerts, and teaching, in addition to the regular work with the orchestra, the profession offers a good living. There are now many sophisticated conservatories, universities, and summer music centers that produce highly trained musicians who also have musical knowledge. Even the most recent graduate has had, in addition to his formal training, the opportunity to have heard a broad range of music via records, tapes, live performances, broadcasts, and television. The technical virtuosity of American orchestra members has reached a far higher standard than ever before. When Joseph Silverstein auditioned for the position of concertmaster in 1959, there were ten members of the violin section who auditioned. They all had the technical facility and musical knowledge to play the solo part of Sibelius's Violin Concerto. At the time it was written, some fifty years before, there were not ten violinists in the world who would have attempted it.

The personality cult of conductors prevalent during the 1930s and 1940s, which included the American careers of Koussevitzky, Toscanini, and Stokowski, was valid and exciting at the time. It no

longer exists.   Nor would it be acceptable to contemporary professional musicians.   Conductors are still personalities.   Certainly they
no longer represent father figures, but as individuals they can and
often do have a marked effect on their orchestras.

Seiji Ozawa is very much a man of his time.   When he greeted
the orchestra at his first rehearsal as its new music director, he said
simply, "And now we will make music together."   His rehearsals
are workmanlike and informative.   They are the result of careful
preparation.   Four or five days a week, no matter where he is, he
gets up at four o'clock in the morning and for the next five hours
studies the scores.   If it is a work he has not previously performed,
he uses just the score.   Later he uses the piano as well.   He studies
the score until he knows it so well that he feels he has composed
the music himself.   In that process of possession he has also committed it to memory.   For him memorizing is not a separate process
or something that concerns him.

Even though he goes to rehearsals well prepared, he says there
are often surprises when he conducts music he has previously only
studied.   A wind player may have to tell him that a certain passage
is not possible the way he requests because at a certain point he
will have to take a breath.

Ozawa enjoys the discussion of the music and its performance
with the musicians.   He recognizes their superb technical skill and
knows that they enjoy playing a variety of music.   "A new score
every day is what they would really like.   That is hard on the conductor," he said.   Ozawa's understanding, respect, and concern for
the intellectual stimulation and enjoyment of the musicians is a
very different view of them from that held by previous generations
of conductors.   It is the serious recognition of a unique mutual
effort.   The nature of this effort is best described in its absence by
the great Spanish violinist Pablo de Sarasate talking to a friend,
composer Enrique Granados, during the late 1800s:

> Enrique, do you know what is happening today?   I mean these
> conductors, with their little sticks.   They don't play, you know.
> They stand in front of the orchestra waving their little sticks.   And
> they get paid for this, get paid well, too.   Now suppose, Enrique,
> suppose there were no orchestra and they stood alone.   Would they
> pay them just the same — them and their little sticks?

Chapter Six

Orchestral Music
and Musicians

"Sixty years ago I wished to be a musician, and therefor went to Vienna, where I studied two years and half diligently, learned something of music, something about musicians, and one other thing — that I had no talent for music."　　— Major Higginson

GEORGE BERNARD SHAW once wrote: "Orchestras only need to be sworn at and a German is consequently at an advantage with them, as English profanity, except in America, has not gone beyond a limited technology of perdition."

Disregarding what Shaw was saying about the English language, his view does reflect the low esteem in which musicians have been held even until recent years. The Boston Symphony Orchestra, with its consistent level of performance, highly trained musicians, gifted conductors, and loyal trustees and administrative staffs, evolved from a simpler time and the private needs of individuals.

In early times there were just three reasons to hire a musician: for dancing, for a church service, or to accompany the marching of soldiers. For centuries prior to the formation of orchestras musicians had been itinerant entertainers, working where they could, receiving meager wages, and generally considered to be undesirable members of society. Early instrumental music was listened to only as the accompaniment to another activity, and little has been written about its performers. But we do know that Henry VIII had an orchestra that included 614 strings and 215 wind instruments to accompany the functions of his court.

Queen Elizabeth maintained an orchestra of forty for the same purpose.   Beginning in the sixteenth century, the kings of France retained two bands, one known as the Petite, which was a string orchestra and played "aristocratic" music for the court; and a second, the Grande, which consisted of oboes, trumpets, trombones, and drums, and played popular dances for the people.

None of the instruments common before 1600 exists now in its original form.   There were no standard sizes for stringed instruments; wind instruments had no valves, so notes were approximately reached rather than accurately played.   In the early notation of music there was no distinction between vocal and instrumental literature.   Only notes were written and they were performed as well as possible, either by voices or by instruments.   Some early orchestras such as Bach's grew up imitating the sound of the organ. The making of music, both its composition and its performance, was considered to be a craft and was passed from father to son and taught by apprenticeship.   Advanced musical training in the seventeenth and eighteenth centuries was available only in Italy at the Venetian and Neapolitan conservatories, which were religious institutions.   Few could take advantage of this training; Haydn and Bach were among those who could not.

The most regular employment for a musician during the seventeenth and eighteenth centuries was in the courts of archbishops,

Pierre Monteux with the orchestra in 1919.   Fredric Fradkin was then concertmaster.

royalty, and nobility. At those courts the musicians performed the dual role of servant and musician. They were salaried and liveried, often boarded and lodged, sometimes tenured for life, but always at the beck and call of their master. On a moment's notice they played in the church, at the opera, in the theater, for dancing, at open-air serenades, at meals, and if the patron could not sleep they played quietly all night.

The contracts that musicians had with their employers placed great emphasis on the behavior of the musician. In Bach's contract as organist, dated June 15, 1707, at Muhlhausen, Imperial Free City of the Holy Empire, he was required to

> show himself willing in the execution of the duties required of him and be available at all times, particularly attend to his service faithfully and industriously on Sundays, Feast Days and other Holy Days, keep the organ entrusted to him at least in good condition, call attention of those serving at any time as the appointed supervisors to any defects found in it and industriously watch over its repairs and music, be zealous in observing all requirements of a decent and respectful life, also avoid unseemly society and suspicious companie [sic].

His payment consisted of a nominal amount of money, grain, and some wood, either oak or ash, for his fire.

Koussevitzky with the orchestra in Symphony Hall.

Bach was notorious for getting into arguments with his employers and with musicians who could not play as well as he demanded. Once, in a rage at an incompetent musician, Bach flung his wig at the offending man's feet and told him he should have been a shoemaker. He objected often and in long letters to his employers about poor pay, the difficulty of maintaining the instruments, and his hopes for finding employment "without further vexation." His employers too complained, "for if he considers it no disgrace to be connected with the Church and to accept his salary, he must not be ashamed to make music with the students assigned to do so." Bach was not the only one reproved, however. On several occasions the choir leader received punishment "for going into the wine cellar on the last preceding Sunday during the sermon."

The Baroque orchestra reflected the splendor, extravagance, and invention of the period. The Handel Commemoration Festival Orchestra at London's Westminster Abbey in 1784 created a very different balance of sound from what we hear today: there were 6 flutes, 26 oboes, 26 bassoons, 48 first violins, 47 second violins, 26 violas, 21 cellos, 15 double basses, 12 trumpets, 12 horns, and 6 trombones.   The size and content of the orchestras depended largely on what musicians were available at the time.   Out of the inventiveness of the Baroque period came new effects.   Instruments that had previously been used only to imitate the sounds of the voice or organ were discovered to have their own qualities and effects.   From this knowledge came the concept of the modern orchestra: instruments accompanying instruments.   Music began to be written that was suitable for no other expression than by an orchestra, and the use of the orchestra was no longer limited to being the servant of some other musical purpose.

The symphony as a musical form marks the beginning of the modern orchestra's career.   The first master of the symphony was Franz Joseph Haydn, who has a pivotal position in the history of music.   During his lifetime Bach was at the height of his career.   Mozart knew, loved, and survived him by eighteen years.   When Haydn died in 1809, Beethoven was forty and had already composed a large part of his life's work.

Haydn was self-taught.   He had been a Vienna choir boy who, in boredom during a church service, once cut off the tail of the wig of the boy standing in front of him.   Like all the contemporary musicians, he lived from one job to the next.   Haydn was a facile composer and wrote whatever was commissioned.   Asked once why he had never composed any quintets, he replied that no one had ever ordered any.   Haydn's reputation grew as his music became known.   As a result, he was hired by Prince Esterházy, in whose service he remained for almost thirty years.   His fame soon spread and he was respected and admired.   Nevertheless, his was a subservient position.   Not only was he "under obligation to compose such music as his Serene Highness may command," the contract also required Haydn to

> conduct himself in an exemplary manner, abstaining from undue familiarity and from vulgarity in eating, drinking, and conversation not dispensing with the respect due to him, but acting uprightly and influencing his subordinates to preserve such harmony as is becoming in them, remembering how displeasing the consequences

of any discord or dispute would be to his Serene Highness . . . [He]
and all his musicians shall appear in uniform, and appear in white
stockings, white linen, powdered, and with either a queue or a
wig.

Composer, musician, and servant were often one and the same
person, and an individual's high or low rank depended upon the
emphasis given to music in the particular establishment where he
worked.

The music of the seventeenth and eighteenth centuries is that of
court composers all over Europe who wrote not for posterity but for
the next performance or the next religious festival. A voluminous
amount of music was written during the period, partly because no
prior repertory existed, but mainly because the splendor and brilliance of the courts relied in large measure on the continuing flow
of new compositions and productions. The object of the music of
the period was to please and to entertain. Music and education
had not yet met; the difference between light and serious music did
not exist. Composers gained prestige and fame from having their
music become popular — it was how they kept their jobs. Haydn
was a genius. But that he wrote one hundred and four symphonies
also shows his need to please. The music of the period was occasional music, much of which served its purpose at the time and has
since been forgotten.

Standards of orchestral playing were at best uneven. In the Italian opera houses it was the expressed duty of the orchestras to
follow the singer, but there was no such thing as a soft accompaniment. In the eyes of the musicians such playing would indicate
that they were incompetent. So each musician played as loudly as
he could. During recitatives, when they were not playing, they
talked to each other and tuned their instruments. Orchestras varied greatly in quality. In 1763 Mozart's father wrote that the
orchestra at Mannheim was "undeniably the best in Europe. It
consists altogether of people who are young and of good character,
not drunkards, gamblers or dissolute fellows, so that both their
behavior and their playing are admirable." This was in contrast to
his assessment of the Salzburg Orchestra: "These are coarse, slov-
enly, dissolute court musicians."

Georg Sievers, a German correspondent to several publications, who lived in Italy in the 1820s and 1830s, wrote this about the opera orchestra:

> During the recitations the players creep under the seats of the orchestra to chat with one another, take a gram of snuff, or even play a practical joke on one of their colleagues. When the leader bangs on the candleholder, they rush out in all directions, two thirds of them usually too late, because in haste one has knocked over a stand, another a candleholder, another the music, or has stepped on a colleague's corn and stops to have an argument with him. In Paris the players are not allowed to leave their seats except in cases of the utmost necessity. The Italian musicians, who take good care of their heads, all wear red caps, which makes them look like the French revolutionaries of 1790.

Berlioz, in Italy at approximately the same time, wrote that the

> [musicians'] wretched blowing and scraping, as indifferent to what is being shouted on stage as to what is buzzed in the boxes and parterre, [are] possessed of but one thought — that of earning their supper. The assemblage of these poor creatures constitutes what is called an orchestra.

On the other hand, Haydn's orchestra was well trained and justly famous. Its members were required to do some domestic chores and, although the subservient role was expected, it was also resented. In 1772 Haydn's orchestra, with the help of its conductor, was the first to demand actively that its contract be honored precisely. Each spring the prince's household moved from Vienna to the country for the summer months. The orchestra members, singers, actors, painters, copyists, and some of the domestic servants had to live in one building, an arrangement that required two or three people to share a room. Because of the crowded quarters the prince gave strict instructions that no musician was to bring his family to Esterházy, and the musicians were paid a little more during the summer months to cover the expenses of two households. But the prince loved his palace in the country, and he stayed on past the agreed-upon summer months into the fall. The musicians complained to Haydn, who tried to intercede with the prince but was turned down. As the weeks went by they asked Haydn to help them. In compliance, he wrote a symphony that surely constitutes the first musicians' strike, the Farewell Symphony. In its last movement each musician stopped playing, one after the other, took his music, instrument, and candle, and left the stage. The closing bars of the symphony were played by the solitary leader of the orchestra. Then he too took his violin, music, and candle and left. The prince was no doubt entertained by the elegance of the pantomime but he understood and gave the order to return to Vienna immediately.

Musicians generally had few recourses in situations like this. They either worked or did not work. They were not part of institutions with long-range artistic goals or plans that even required their participation. It was many years before musicians had any sense of stability; this only occurred with the development of orchestral playing and with the establishment of institutions for the public performance of music, which happened over a period of years. In the eighteenth and nineteenth centuries there was no such thing as full-time employment for a musician with one organization. Musi-

The BSO in costume plays Mozart's *Musical Joke* in the sixties.

cians played when and where there was work, and often they participated in several orchestras in the same city. The number of rehearsals and who attended them varied. It was not unusual for a musician to attend a rehearsal, yet be at another job at the time of the concert. Someone else would play in the actual concert without benefit of prior rehearsal.

Authority and discipline were not regulated, and some orchestras resented the unconditional power of their conductors. It seems to have been characteristic of the first generation of conductors that they were tyrannical, arrogant, and vain. It was not unheard of for musicians to refuse to play for conductors or, perhaps worse, to play but make an impossible situation, such as one time when Beethoven was scheduled to be the soloist in one of his piano concertos. After a particularly brutal rehearsal, the orchestra had refused to play for the scheduled conductor. Beethoven offered to conduct from the piano. Evidently the musicians took out their anger on the composer. A contemporary report describes the performance: "The players did not bother to pay attention to the soloist. As a result there was no delicacy at all to the accompaniment and no response to the musical feeling of the solo player." At the première of his Fifth and Sixth symphonies the orchestra refused to play under Beethoven's stormy direction. In Düsseldorf in the 1830s the players were notorious for getting drunk and fighting. Their conductor at the time was gentle Mendelssohn. Even he lost his temper and screamed at them. In London it was generally known that Covent Garden's Saturday evening performance was to be avoided, as the musicians were paid that day and invariably got drunk in time for the performance, which was of course a shambles.

Europe in the nineteenth century was in a constant state of political, economic, and social upheaval. During revolutions, if an army needed to use an opera house to store food for the winter, music waited. Musicians traveled from city to city and to neighboring countries for work. The variety of sponsoring organizations and societies for the performance of music reflected this turmoil. Some court-sponsored opera houses and their orchestras survived, and there were new, privately supported musical societies.

Musical instruments had become more adaptable. The entire range of brass and woodwinds was equipped with valves, which afforded new possibilities for technical prowess to musicians as well as opportunity for invention to composers. The music of the eighteenth century had had a strong, regular beat to it, and the players had had little trouble keeping together. The music of the nineteenth century offered more challenges. The rational quality and the grace of the music in Haydn's time gave way to the dynamic, emotional qualities of the works by Beethoven and those who followed him. Beethoven was indeed a revolutionary. The drawing rooms of the nobility proved too small for the orchestras that were called upon to play the new music. Concert halls were built across Europe; Paris built its first one in 1831. Orchestral concerts became public affairs regulated by business and attended in large part by the emerging, enthusiastic middle class.

Beginning with Beethoven, composers became more and more concerned with expressions of feelings, musical ideas, and the dynamic effects of sound. With the increased complexity of the music and the demands on the players, amateur musicians who had formerly participated in most orchestras began to fade from the ranks and the role of the conductor became more defined and important.

In the eighteenth century music education was available to the rich as well as to the talented poor, who received their training as apprentices in the courts of princes and archbishops. With the general, growing interest in music and the rapidly increasing number of concerts, a new and appropriate method of training for musicians was needed in the nineteenth century.

The Paris Conservatory, founded by the government in 1793, became the model. In the early 1800s it provided, on a democratic basis, free training to gifted pupils who were admitted by audition. This new form of music education took hold quickly. In the first decades of the 1800s conservatories functioning under similar principles sprang up in the major cities of Europe: Milan, 1807; Naples, 1808; Prague, 1811; Brussels, 1813; Florence, 1814; Vienna, 1817; London, 1822; and Leipzig, 1843. It was from these conservatories that the next and future generations of musicians and conductors would come. The establishment of these conservatories marked the advent of the professional status of musicians. But it took almost one hundred years for the image of the itinerant, talented servants to be replaced by that of today's highly trained musicians, who are

Erich Leinsdorf asks the orchestra "to sing."

recognized as being on an equal footing with other professionals
who also require special gifts and extensive training. Clearly, at
the turn of the century, George Bernard Shaw was not yet impressed. But at the time Henry Higginson traveled around Europe
and visited in Vienna in the late 1850s, the effect of the conservatory training was being felt in orchestras, and the standards of
musical performances had changed accordingly.

New ideas and new forms of music were not easily accepted by
orchestras, and von Bülow's highly trained, magnificent orchestra
in Mannheim was the result of ten hours of daily rehearsal. Wagner's orchestra, which included Nikisch as violinist, resented his
rehearsing each section of the orchestra separately for the Beethoven Ninth. But after the first full rehearsal they understood and
cheered him spontaneously.

During the continuing upheavals and revolutions of Europe, music became one of the dominant art forms, the international language of pleasure, and the expression of hope and freedom. Music
was no longer played for the pleasure of the aristocracy alone. A

concert was an opportunity to hear new compositions written especially for the general public. This music, to achieve its full effect, required neither a drawing room nor a church, but a large civic center filled with excited responsive people. These concerts were of interest not only to the growing number of music lovers who attended, but also to those who wished only to be well informed. Even without electrical and technical contrivances, word traveled swiftly through Europe and the merits of the newest compositions of Schumann, Brahms, Berlioz, Chopin, Mendelssohn, Wagner, and any number of composers all of the same period were hotly discussed. Orchestras, both professional and amateur, sprang up in even the smallest cities and towns. Chamber music was played in homes, and the process of making music became obsessive and absorbed people in the way it did young Henry Higginson during his years in Vienna.

In these tense years emotions ran high, and audiences were as vociferous in their disgust as they were ebullient in their praise of new compositions and performances of technical virtuosity. Music and revolution touched many lives, sometimes simultaneously. In his memoirs, Berlioz, whose *Symphonie Fantastique* had already been performed with success, describes a scene in Paris during the July Revolution of 1830:

> I had a musical experience — shock would almost be a better word — of extraordinary intensity. I was crossing the courtyard of the Palais Royal when I thought I heard a tune that I knew well; it seemed to be coming from a group of people on the far side. I went towards them and perceived that a dozen or so young men were engaged in singing a battle hymn of my composition . . . Unused as I was to this kind of popularity, the discovery delighted me and I pushed my way through to the circle of singers and requested permission to join them. It was granted and I was handed a copy of the bass part — which in the case of this particular chorus was quite superfluous. I was careful, however, not to betray my identity, though I remember having a lively argument with the conductor over the tempo at which he was taking my piece . . . During the intervals in this improvised concert three National Guardsmen, who were keeping the crowd clear of the singers, handed round their shakos and made a collection for the people wounded during the Three Days. The idea appealed to the Parisian sense of the bizarre, and there was soon a deluge of five-franc pieces which our

music by itself would hardly have been enough to charm from their owners' pockets. The audience grew steadily and the space round the little patriotic band got smaller and smaller. Our military escort began to lose all hope of stemming the tide. We barely escaped, and fled with the crowd streaming behind us till we reached the Galerie Colbert which leads to the rue Vivienne. There, surrounded and hemmed in like bears at a fair, we were invited to resume our singing. A haberdasher, whose shop opened off the glass-covered central area of the arcade, asked us up to the first floor, where we could "rain down our music on our admirers" without risk of being suffocated. The offer was accepted, and we struck up the Marseillaise. Almost at once the seething mass at our feet grew quiet and a holy stillness fell upon them. It was like the silence in St. Peter's Square when the Pope gives his blessing, *urbi et orbi*, from the pontifical balcony. At the end of the second verse, at the point where the refrain enters, there was again a profound silence. It was the same after the third. This was not at all what I had expected. On beholding that vast concourse of people I recalled that I had just arranged Rouget de Lisle's song [the Marseillaise] for double chorus and full orchestra, and that where one normally writes "tenors and basses" I had written instead "everyone with a voice, a soul, and blood in his veins." This seemed just the occasion for it; so it was all the more mortifying to be met with a stubborn silence. The fourth time, I could contain myself no longer, and as the verse came to an end I yelled, "Confound it all — sing!" The great crowd roared out its *"Aux armes, citoyens!"* with the power and precision of a trained choir. Remember that the arcade leading to the rue Vivienne was packed with people, as was the arcade leading to the rue Neuve-des-Petits-Champs and the central area under the dome, and that these four or five thousand voices were crammed into a resonant space bounded by the clapboards and shutters of the shops, the glass of the roof and the flagstones of the arcades. Remember too that most of them, men, women and children, were hot from the barricades, their pulses still throbbing with the excitement of the recent struggle, and then try to imagine the effect of this stupendous refrain. I literally sank to the floor, while our little band, aghast at the explosion it had provoked, stood dumbfounded, silent as birds after a thunderclap.

One of the results of Europe's upheavals was a steady stream of immigrants to America. Among these were well-trained musicians and of course the entire Germania Orchestra, which arrived in

1848. Musical performances by this country's early settlers had focused on religious works and the music societies were comprised largely of amateur musicians. Musical resources were meager in the cities of the United States. In 1823 the drums owned by the Handel and Haydn Society of Boston were loaned to the New York Choral Society for a performance in New York of Beethoven's *Mount of Olives*. In 1829 a contemporary account describes the musical poverty of the New York theaters and operas:

> The orchestras are extremely bad and incomplete. There are seldom two clarionets, and generally no bassoon. Oboes, trumpets and drums are never to be met with. Oboes are almost unknown in this country; in the whole of North America there is only one player, who lives in Baltimore. Notwithstanding the imperfection of their orchestras, they play the sinfonias of Haydn; and although the want of instruments often brings them to a stand-still, they treat the silence as if it were a pause, and play on. In every orchestra there is a trombone, which never plays its part, but generally that of the violoncello; and if the performer is skillful enough, he sometimes plays that of the violin. Trombones and double basses are best paid; they receive $16 or $17 a week; the others have but $10 or $12; the best clarionet has $15. They play every day except Sunday, commencing at half-past eight, and ending about one o'clock in the morning.

The fact that only a few years later Theodore Thomas, himself trained in Germany, was able to put together an orchestra and tour the country is testament to his own missionary zeal as well as to the growing interest in classical music in this country.

The orchestra of the Grand Opera in New York in 1850 included twenty-seven Bohemians, twelve Germans, nine Frenchmen, eight Englishmen, seven Italians, four Spaniards, two Hungarians, one Pole, one Portuguese, and one African Negro, "who beats the big drum."

Toward the end of the century institutions were founded in this country and Europe to give some permanence and stability to the performance of music. Both in England and America musicians were among the first working groups to unionize in order to establish some regulation and uniformity as to fees, contracts, and conditions of employment. All the early orchestras in this country were as cosmopolitan in their make-up as New York's Grand Opera

Orchestra. Thus, it was most natural for Major Higginson and conductor Wilhelm Gericke to turn to the conservatory-trained musicians of Europe at the close of the Boston orchestra's fourth season. The experienced musicians who were familiar with the repertory have always been a crucial ingredient in the success of the orchestra, especially in its early days. At the beginning of the fifth season there were twenty new members, none of whom spoke English. A facetious critic at Thanksgiving that year suggested that a rival orchestra might be set up by those who had been let go. And in his list of things Bostonians should be thankful for he included that "Mr. Gericke in his sweeping discharges, did not also include Major Higginson and that one or two Americans are still left in our Symphony Orchestra, so that the United States' language might be protected from oblivion."

When Muck became conductor, many of the new musicians came from Berlin at his request to be part of the orchestra here. Arthur Fiedler, who joined the orchestra at Muck's invitation in 1915, was one of the orchestra's eight native-born Americans, but even he had received his training at the Berlin Conservatory. After the first year of Koussevitzky's tenure, many members of his Concerts Koussevitzky in Paris joined the Boston Symphony. There are fewer foreign-born members in the orchestra currently. But it has remained more cosmopolitan than most other symphony orchestras in the country. This has had a marked effect on it, one that is noticeable still. For musicians coming from abroad who could not yet speak English, the orchestra became their only community. Fellow musicians also from abroad were their first friends — they saw each other's families and played chamber music together. This sense of community differentiates the Boston Symphony from other American orchestras, which, like Boston's, are highly professional but lack the added dimension of this particular sense of unity. Previous conductors have remarked on this characteristic, but Ozawa feels especially strongly that this unique quality continues to enhance the sound and the pleasure of the Boston orchestra's performances.

The first year of the Boston Symphony concerts, 1881, the composition of the orchestra was:
First violins, 13; second violins, 11; violas, 10; cellos, 8; double basses, 8; flutes, 2; oboes, 2; clarinets, 2; bassoons, 2; contrabas-

soon, 1; horns, 4; trumpets, 2; trombones, 3; tuba, 1; timpani, 1; harp, 1. Total: 72.

In its fiftieth season, under Koussevitzky, it was:
First violins, 18; second violins, 16; violas, 13; cellos, 10; basses, 10; flutes, 4; oboes, 3; clarinets, 4; bassoons, 4; English horn, 1; bass clarinet, 1; contrabassoon, 1; horns, 8; trumpets, 6; trombones, 4; tuba, 1; harps, 2; timpani, 2; percussion, 3; organ, 1; librarian, 1. Total: 113.

And in its ninety-sixth season, under Seiji Ozawa, it was:
First violins, 18; second violins, 15; violas, 12; cellos, 11; basses, 9; flutes, 3; piccolo, 1; oboes, 2; English horn, 1; clarinets, 3; bass clarinet, 1; bassoons, 3; contrabassoon, 1; horns, 6; trumpets, 4; trombones, 4; tuba, 1; timpani, 1; percussion, 4; harps, 2; librarians, 2. Total: 104.

Looking at the make-up of the orchestra at fifty-year intervals is revealing. The lists of instruments and number of players give no indication of the continuing evolution of the language of music, particularly of the last fifty years. To the casual observer, the orchestra remains a nineteenth-century invention. Most of its repertory was composed in the 1800s, although music from the seventeenth and eighteenth centuries and sometimes from the twentieth is programmed as well. However, much of the most current music is very difficult and complicated to perform, and, as in the past, the avant-garde has always had to fight for survival and recognition and it takes a dynamic promoter to achieve consistent performance of contemporary works. Although he himself preferred nineteenth-century music, Major Higginson understood that the promotion of contemporary music was a part of his responsibility as benefactor of the orchestra. Monteux relentlessly pursued the avant-garde; Koussevitzky did so flamboyantly and with complete dedication. He provided funds to commission new works and often guaranteed their publication.

Until 1942, when the orchestra joined the union, rehearsals could continue as long as the conductor wished. Now, with a limited amount of rehearsal time available and the demands of contemporary scores, it becomes exorbitantly expensive and often initially unrewarding for conductors and orchestras to perform new works, and so the opportunity to hear new works is becoming rare. The

Seiji Ozawa in concert.

Spectrum Series of concerts by the Boston Symphony, under the direction of the young conductor Michael Tilson Thomas, was scheduled for the specific purpose of performing new works during the seasons 1971–1973. The audiences were not large, and the series was ultimately discontinued. Although new works *are* performed by the orchestra, it may well be that it is no longer financially possible for orchestras to promote the most contemporary music. Much of the new music that is performed today is played by smaller groups, for whom the costs of rehearsal and performance are not so high. The National Endowment for the Arts, the government agency for the encouragement and support of the arts in this country, is now assuming part of the role of promoter of contemporary American music together with private foundation support organized expressly for that purpose.

Onstage, any orchestra will always look like a nineteenth-century institution. Until the middle of the twentieth century, this musical organization had no difficulty in being a part of the contemporary scene. Since then and because of a variety of pressures it has become increasingly difficult for large, established orchestras to keep pace with the music of contemporary composers.

Chapter Seven

Making Music Together

*"If the world consisted only of musicians, it would go to pieces at
once!"*
— Major Higginson

MAJOR HIGGINSON PLACED the artistic direction of the Boston
Symphony in the hands of the conductor, but as its patron he participated directly in all functions of the orchestra as he saw fit. At
the end of each season he gathered the musicians together in the
Green Room and congratulated them on a fine season. He would
say, "You have worked hard for your money and you have played
well. Next year you will play even better."

His office downtown was always open to the musicians, and he
was as interested in their economics as in his own. Sometimes he
suggested ways that they might invest their earnings. His ritual
upon arrival at the office included checking on the mail immediately, not only to discover its contents, but also to see if any stamps
remained uncanceled and thus could be steamed off and used
again. Later that same day he might well give $50,000 to a hospital
or a university, but as a private person he was a frugal man. He
would instruct the musicians not to buy new shoes but to have
theirs resoled, pointing out that his had been so treated three or
four times.

Not only did he search personally for conductors at the appropriate times, he also recruited musicians from Europe. On a trip to
Paris in 1912 Major Higginson made an appointment with Fernand
Gillet, the first oboist of the Paris Opéra and Concerts Lamoureux.
Gillet had no idea who Major Higginson was, but he dutifully presented himself at the appointed hour. Major Higginson was frank
and to the point: "I am worried about M. Longy, the first oboist of

the Boston Symphony who has been with the Orchestra since 1898 and who plays so beautifully. He is getting so fat that I think he might burst. I would like you to come to Boston and play second oboe so that if he does, you will be there to take over." Gillet replied that he played first oboe, and that when there was an opening for the first chair they should talk again. Then out of curiosity he asked, "Who are you? Are you the conductor?"

"No," replied Major Higginson. "I'm nobody at all. I just pay the bills."

Longy did not burst and he did not leave until twelve years later, after Koussevitzky's first season. Fernand Gillet, with sixteen others mostly from Paris, then joined the Boston Symphony.

Whenever a new conductor takes over an orchestra there are changes in its personnel. This is partly because it is an appropriate opportunity for some of the older members to retire and a natural break for others to move on. The sound of any orchestra is developed from its dominant players, and the assignment of those key positions is one of the ways a conductor has of achieving the results he wants. It is perhaps typical for a conductor who takes over a new orchestra to feel in some measure what Gericke expressed when he said to Major Higginson when he came to Boston in 1884, "You have some musicians here but it is hardly an orchestra." Every conductor has a natural desire to place his personal stamp on his orchestra. During his first season in particular Gericke's aim was to form a cohesive unit for regular performance. Musicians had been used to making a living by playing wherever a job was available. The idea that players would contract to perform under a single conductor and with a single orchestra was a novel concept. Indeed, it was Major Higginson who defined the idea of a single team of players, which became the foundation of all American orchestras. A musician's personal contract with Major Higginson to play in the Boston Symphony looked like this:

BOSTON, Feb. 25, 1882

Mr. ———

DEAR SIR —— I wish to engage you for the next season as . . . under the following conditions:

I. The Orchestra will have as conductor, Mr. George Henschel, and as leader, Mr. Bernhard Listemann.

II. Your services will be required on each week, between October 1 and April 1, on the following days: Wednesday morning, afternoon and evening; Thursday morning, afternoon and evening; Friday morning and afternoon; Saturday morning and evening.

III. On Wednesday and Thursday all your time will, of course, not be required, but you must be ready when needed. You will be expected to play during these four days either at concerts or at rehearsals, as required. If it is necessary to give a concert occasionally on Friday you will be asked to give that evening in place of another.

IV. On the days specified you will neither play in any other orchestra nor under any other conductor than Mr. Henschel, except if wanted in your leisure hours by the Handel and Haydn Society, nor will you play for dancing.

V. I offer . . . weekly, and also your expenses when travelling on business of the Orchestra.

It is the intention, if the circumstances are as favorable as at present, to make this a permanent orchestra of the highest order.

Its success will depend very greatly on your efforts and on your cooperation.

I wish to offer my sincere thanks for your labor and zeal during the present season, and hope for your services in the next.

In order to facilitate the needed arrangements, your answer is expected by March 2.

Yours truly

Henry L. Higginson

The building of the orchestra was not an easy task, even with trained musicians from Europe to help. Gericke described some of the problems in a letter:

When the second season [Gericke's, 1885–1886] with the new members began, I had hoped the fresh element would make my work easier, and heighten our success; but I was mistaken. I soon felt that all the twenty dismissed members, with their families, were like millstones round my neck. The remaining old members took the part of the dismissed ones, opposed me where they could, and put themselves into direct opposition; a great part of the audience, even some of the critics, were influenced for the same reason. I was not popular in the Orchestra, especially as they did not yet understand why I should ask for better playing and more exact work than had been done heretofore. Before I came to Boston, the members of the Orchestra had been used to a great deal of freedom; for instance, members living out of town were allowed to leave the rehearsal at twelve in order to be home for lunch; or, to reach a train for another out-of-town engagement of their own — whether the rehearsal was finished or not. It was not easy to make them understand that their engagement for the Boston Symphony Concerts had to be considered first and foremost, and that the rehearsal had to be finished before everything else. It took Mr. Higginson's whole energy to make them understand that they had to consider me in this way and rehearse and play as satisfactorily as I thought it necessary.

The end of the second season, however, brought a great change. We made our first *tournée* to different cities, and at this time in Philadelphia the Orchestra earned there its first real success. The musicians began to understand what the hard work and earnest study had meant, and what results were reached by it; it opened their eyes and gave them a feeling of pride and satisfaction with themselves.

In the early days of the orchestra the usual way for musicians to be hired was on the basis of word-of-mouth recommendation. Then an invitation was extended, as in the case of Fernand Gillet. In the time of Monteux and Koussevitzky, extensive auditioning was required. In 1930, for example, there was an opening for third trumpet. René Voisin thought it would be a good opportunity for his fifteen-and-a-half-year-old son and student, Roger, and he encouraged him to audition. Roger played everything well and easily. Koussevitzky asked him to play the note "la," and told him where on the register he wanted the "la." He asked him to start softly, then make a crescendo, then slowly fade the note completely. Young Roger understood the directions and did as he was told just perfectly. It wasn't until later that he realized that Koussevitzky had asked him to play the treacherously difficult opening of Wagner's *Rienzi* Overture, a work known to make trumpeters break out in a cold sweat at the very thought of the technical challenges. Roger was hired and joined the orchestra that fall at age sixteen, its youngest member. For the next twenty years Roger sat next to his father, who had joined the orchestra two years before, when the family came from France. They were the only father and son team to play together in the orchestra, although there was a time when it had as many as four Fiedlers, one of whom was Arthur, the others his relatives.

During Koussevitzky's tenure the audition process became more formal. There were complaints from professional musicians that students from Tanglewood appeared mysteriously in the ranks of the orchestra at Symphony Hall in the autumn, having been privately invited by the conductor. And Koussevitzky was notorious for making promises that were not always kept. Each composer was promised a performance, and young musicians were led to expect a place in his orchestra. As he told a friend, "I have the weakness to make many promises, but I have the strength not to keep them." When Charles Munch became music director screens were used for the initial auditions in order to make the competition more democratic. And the personnel manager thoughtfully suggested that ladies take off their high heels so that their footsteps would not betray their sex. It is now the custom that when the audition process has eliminated all but ten, the conductor joins the jury of orchestra members and the screens are removed. However, in the case of violin players, the present concertmaster, Joseph Silverstein, prefers the screen to remain, as frequently his own students are auditioning. In 1977 five of his former students played in the orchestra.

Naturally enough, most musicians are nervous before auditioning. A few are not. Charles Munch sat with his first-chair players at an audition in New York for a new clarinetist. Jovial Gino Cioffi came in beaming, wished everyone good-morning, and asked what they would like to hear. Munch politely asked what he had prepared for the occasion. Cioffi responded expansively that he was ready to play anything they wanted to hear — concerto, symphony, opera. Munch suggested the Mozart Clarinet Concerto. Cioffi played the first movement with elegance and brilliance, ending in a dazzling display of virtuosity. Obviously pleased with himself, he leaned toward Munch. "Pretty good, uh?" He was hired immediately.

However, Cioffi's thick accent got him in trouble on more than one occasion. When Toscanini's protégé Guido Cantelli came to Boston to conduct the Verdi *Requiem*, he and Cioffi had some discussion about whether a note was actually F-sharp or F "natch."

Cantelli stormed off the stage, complaining of insubordination and insisting, "Thata man's a-immatata me." Cioffi was also the source of much merriment within the orchestra. Once a student was having trouble coming in at the right moment. Cioffi was impatient: "One-a, two-a, play." Again the student waited too long, explaining that his way made the music more interesting. Furious, Cioffi said, "Whadda you thinka music is, you gotta dressa it upa, a lamba chop?"

In Europe, where there is a tradition of sovereignty and dictatorship, orchestras are frequently cooperatives. In America orchestras represent an interesting dichotomy. They are essentially autocratic institutions functioning in a democratic society. The orchestra's history parallels that of the industrial revolution. It is not difficult to see an orchestra as a giant precision instrument that can generate excitement just from its sheer power and accuracy. To watch and listen to a good orchestra play even second-rate music superbly can be an awesome experience. Since musicians saw themselves as a work force and organized their union in the late nineteenth century, the community of musicians revolves around each orchestra's committee, which negotiates the terms of its contract with manage-

Joseph Silverstein, concertmaster, instructs students at the Berkshire Music Festival.

ment. These committees have recently won the right to participate in some artistic decisions. For example, committee members may be part of the jury at auditions and may make suggestions about guest conductors.

It is hard for soldiers to take power away from their general. The same is true for musicians. As a result of years of tyrannical conductors, insensitive management, and trustees who had little regard for musicians, the committees in many American orchestras have made fierce demands and have reached for power in retaliation for the injustices of the past. One orchestra went so far as to demand that it be written into the contract that the conductor might not frown at the players during rehearsal. When Seiji Ozawa took over the San Francisco Symphony, he tried to assert his right to dismiss two players. The orchestra's committee threatened to resign in a power play and so took away that traditional right of conductors. As time has gone on, many orchestras have found it necessary to strike for higher wages and increased benefits. The Boston Symphony is something of an exception, as its members have not gone on strike since 1920, and the orchestra is proud of the fact that several years ago it played almost an entire season without a contract while negotiations proceeded amicably.

Musicians have as diverse backgrounds and interests as those in any profession. But, unlike most professions, a musician's training must begin at an early age and is separate from the regular school curriculum. In order to sustain the student's interest and concentration during the lengthy, expensive process, expectations for success must be set high. The mother who says of her son, "He is just as good a violinist as Heifetz, but not as lucky," speaks volumes. But while every musician cannot be an internationally acclaimed soloist, it in no way demeans a musician to take up the rewarding professional career of playing in an orchestra.

Joseph Silverstein, concertmaster of the Boston Symphony and a soloist of stature, chose to make his career as an orchestral musician rather than to pursue the more exciting but more hazardous path of soloist, which was certainly within his grasp. Silverstein is a man who has always known his own mind. When at the age of four he was given his first quarter-size violin, he smashed it. He had wanted a piano. When he joined the Boston Symphony in 1955 at twenty-three, he was its youngest member at the time. He was a prizewinner in the 1959 Queen Elizabeth of Belgium International Competition and a year later won the coveted Naumburg Foundation Award. Since then he has become chairman of the faculty at the Berkshire Music Center and associate professor of music at Yale and also at Boston University, where the orchestra he trained and conducted won great honor in Germany during the summer of 1976. And he has appeared regularly as the soloist with the Boston Symphony and in 1971 was appointed its assistant conductor. During William Steinberg's short tenure with the orchestra, Silverstein on occasion conducted for him. In one three-day period Steinberg's doctor would let him conduct only two of the three performances, so Silverstein conducted the third. After the weekend was over Steinberg asked his substitute, "Herr Professor [he always called him that], now you have both played in and conducted the Mahler Fifth, tell me which is easier . . . No, don't tell me or anyone else!"

The job of concertmaster depends on the sophistication of the conductor. If, for instance, the conductor wants a certain effect from the bowing of violins but doesn't know the vocabulary of violin playing, then it is up to the concertmaster to understand and to explain to the violin section what is needed. Some conductors such as Leinsdorf do not correct an individual's errors directly but rather instruct the section leader to make sure the error is corrected. With a conductor such as Monteux, who corrected players kindly and directly, or Munch, who really didn't like to rehearse, the concertmaster's job was to play the solo parts and, as the spokesman or leader of the musicians, to generate and sustain a level of infectious enthusiasm. As a courtesy, Silverstein always stops by the conductor's dressing room before each concert to see if he has any instructions or special needs. In Europe the concertmaster — or leader, as he is called there — walks in alone, to applause, just before the conductor comes in. In this country he comes in with the other musicians, but it is he who quiets the musicians and signals the oboe to play "A" so that they may tune together, thereby readying the orchestra for the conductor. In Koussevitzky's time concertmaster Richard Burgin played an important extramusical role. He understood the vagaries of Koussevitzky's personality and at times acted as a buffer between the orchestra's fiery leader and the musicians.

Burgin was also a conductor in his own right and led the orchestra in many premières of new works, among them Shostakovich's Fifth Symphony. In 1934, when he conducted the orchestra in its first performance of Hindemith's *Mathis der Maler*, he was appointed associate conductor.

Orchestral musicians work as a group. But they are all individuals with expectations of success, and the one thing they find most uncomfortable and insulting is to be treated as a mere *fonctionnaire*, or "doer." An orchestra of the caliber of the Boston Symphony does not play under many second-rate guest conductors, but every so often one does appear. It is easy to tell what is going on from the players' reactions. The musicians become engrossed in their scores even between movements, do a prodigious amount of tuning, and rarely look up at the man who demands so little or who is lost in his own antics. The musicians' reactions to a conductor are usually instantaneous, and they tend to be unanimous. They will never play badly for even the most inept conductor because their own reputation and pride in their orchestra demand that they play well. Three sets of circumstances may occur with an inadequate conductor. The musicians may ignore him, play well, and go home feeling annoyed. If the conductor bothers them too much the orchestra may play mezzo-forte throughout, with no attention to variation or nuance, making all the notes equal in sonority. In France this is called *grève-perlée*, or "a pearled strike." If the conductor is arrogant and lectures endlessly, demeaning or insulting them, the musicians will pay him the greatest insult of all and follow his directions to the note. Within minutes the effort will result in disaster. This has not happened for many, many years, as the Boston Symphony has no need to engage any but top-flight conductors.

Musicians care a great deal about how they play. They wish always to play their very best, and they wish to be corrected. They thrive on being asked to play better. That is how Koussevitzky was able to do what he did. Under his direction the musicians' expectations for success were always met. To them he was a magician — a tyrant, but a magician. He created a certain creative atmosphere and the performances that resulted were colorful and brilliant. It

Colin Davis, the principal guest conductor, with the orchestra *(Michael Pierce).*

can be said that there were no dull or routine concerts under his direction, and the fact that Koussevitzky held the interest and enthusiasm of audiences for twenty-five years speaks for itself. Fernand Gillet, first oboe for twenty-one years under Koussevitzky, described how during that time he must have played the Brahms First Symphony at least forty times. "And it was incredible," he said. "Each time during the coda I always felt a shiver in my spine." Now Gillet, who retired from the orchestra in 1946, is a gentle, very frail old man in his nineties. Sitting in his big comfortable chair, he will raise his fist high above his head and in a whispy voice filled with passion proclaim: "Long live the Koussevitzky memory!"

It is now customary for the music director to take a break of several weeks in the middle of each season to rest and to prepare new works. During that time the orchestra is conducted by guest conductors and its principal guest conductor, Colin Davis, whom the musicians both like and admire. In Koussevitzky's era the orchestra was generally conducted during this hiatus by contemporary composers, who were delighted to have the opportunity to conduct their own music. This arrangement also provided an exciting opportunity for the audience to feel in touch with the creators of music. And for the musicians it was a unique and often demanding experience. Theirs was the pleasure of an intimate association with composers whose musical talents were frequently not best expressed in their conducting. Maurice Ravel was one of the first of these guest conductor–composers, in January 1928. The musicians were intrigued when at the first rehearsal Ravel appeared in a blue shirt and pale blue suspenders. At the second rehearsal he wore a pink shirt with matching suspenders. His program in-

Nadia Boulanger appeared with the orchestra in 1938 and again in the late 1950s.

cluded *Le Tombeau de Couperin*, *Shéhérazade*, *Rhapsodie Espagnole*, and *La Valse*. Although he was not a decisive, forceful conductor, the musicians knew his music, knew what he wanted, and took pleasure in creating a memorable experience for everyone.

Alexander Glazunov, the venerable Russian composer, came to Boston in 1930 to conduct the orchestra. Arthur Fiedler remembers him as "a nice old bear." He was, with Borodin and Rimsky-Korsakov, a link with the past. Fourteen of his compositions had been played by the orchestra since 1897. Koussevitzky proudly took him to the orchestra's library, saying, "Do you see? We have your works!" "Yes," answered Glazunov, unimpressed, "and they are full of dust."

The musicians knew and respected his position in the history of music, more so perhaps than the audience. Glazunov knew little about conducting, but again it did not matter, for the musicians knew his music and the concerts gave him great pleasure. He stood at the podium, a happy old man, beaming and waving his arms more in delight than to convey specific instructions to the musicians.

In 1938 Nadia Boulanger became the first woman to conduct the Boston Symphony, and it was to her that a generation of composers owed their training. Tall and effective, she was matter-of-fact about both her English and her sex. She said, "My English is what it can," and "When I am making my job I do not consider that I am a woman. I was born so and it does not now astonish me." She conducted a performance of the Fauré *Requiem*, which made a deep impression.

Prokofiev came several times, both to conduct and to be the piano soloist. After his Fourth Symphony was not well received in Boston, he vowed that he would play only "children's music" for the unenlightened audience, and he promptly charmed them with *Peter and the Wolf*. Rachmaninoff, too, came, no stranger to Koussevitzky or to Boston. He is remembered by some of today's orchestra players sitting at the piano at rehearsal slightly bemused, always with a cigarette drooping out of the corner of his mouth.

There are some remarks that neither musicians nor anyone else should make to a conductor who does not brook latitudes with his own ideas. With Munch it was: "Don't you think that this is a little

Three composers who also conducted the orchestra: Igor Stravinsky, Alexander Glazunov *(The Bettman Archive, Inc.)*, Maurice Joseph Ravel *(The Bettman Archive, Inc.)*.

Roger Voisin's photograph of Sibelius's house.

fast for this piece?" The invariable response to such a question was an increase in tempo. With Koussevitzky it was: "I don't understand that new work." He would have the musicians play it over until it was understood. In the case of Shostakovich's Fifth Symphony just *because* it had been denounced by the critics, he led repeat performances of it until the critics were forced, publicly, to change their views.

The musicians witness many tense moments in the preparation of new works. After a rehearsal of Ravel's *Mother Goose Suite,* Koussevitzky turned to the composer.

"Well, how do you like it?"

"It is very nice," answered Ravel, "but it is not what I have written."

"No," responded Koussevitzky with delight. "It is better."

Not all composers were happy to have Koussevitzky take such liberties with their music. Hindemith and Roger Sessions were among those who insisted that their music be played exactly as written. But most contemporary composers were grateful for the brilliant performances given by the orchestra. The Boston Symphony musicians in the Koussevitzky years participated in and contributed to a remarkable epoch in the history of orchestral music. There is no doubt that music written during that period was profoundly influenced by the Boston musicians' style, their brilliance, their ensemble, and their command of subtle nuances. Certainly the orchestra was responsible in large part for the immediate success of several composers, such as Aaron Copland. Koussevitzky liked his music and many of Copland's early works were written expressly for the Boston Symphony. Copland has also conducted the orchestra on several occasions. An anecdote illustrates their close relationship. Once Koussevitzky transcribed a Bach toccata, and after its performance he asked Copland, "How do you like my composition?" "How do you like my conducting?" quickly countered the composer. Slowly Koussevitzky replied, "So bad it could not be."

Certain compositions have always had a place in the repertory. Since the orchestra's early years the First and Second of Sibelius's symphonies have been performed regularly. Muck planned to play the Third and then changed his mind. He rehearsed the Fourth eight times and performed it only three. He gave it back to the librarian, saying he was still unclear about the composer's intention. Monteux also rehearsed the Third, announced it, and then withdrew it. Koussevitzky liked it better. In the years between 1925 and 1935 Sibelius's music was played regularly. All seven symphonies were performed as well as the Violin Concerto, with Richard Burgin as the soloist three times and Heifetz once. Koussevitzky was always particularly careful about the performance of Sibelius's music. He once even cabled the composer for instruction concerning the tempo of a particular section. The wise answer may not have been helpful: "Whatever tempo you feel." Plans were made for Sibelius to visit Boston but they never materialized, and neither did the longed-for Eighth Sympony. When the orchestra went on the European tour that included Helsinki, Roger Voisin, one of the fine photographers in the orchestra, received permission from Sibelius's housekeeper to drive out to the house and take photographs of its exterior. He had no expectation of actually meeting the composer, who was a recluse and unwell. Voisin was moving quietly around the outside, taking his photographs, when the door opened and the housekeeper invited him in. Evidently Sibelius had seen Voisin taking the pictures and had noticed that the bag of camera equipment had BOSTON SYMPHONY ORCHESTRA printed on it. Not well enough to attend the concerts in his honor, Sibelius was nevertheless excited and pleased to meet and talk to one of the musicians of the orchestra that had done so much to bring his music to the public's attention. It was a memorable moment for both men. In a mixture of French and English the two conversed warmly, one in admiration of great music, the other in gratitude for fine performances.

On that same tour the orchestra went to the Soviet Union. They were anxious to hear and to talk to musicians there. The recordings that had come out of postwar Russia had led them to believe that musicians there not only had a different system of tuning but even played certain wind instruments differently. The Americans found the condition of the instruments following the treacherous war years so appalling that they were amazed that the Soviets were able to play them at all. The Boston musicians all traveled with plenty of extra parts for emergencies, so they left as many mouthpieces, bridges, reeds, and strings as they could with their grateful Soviet counterparts. In the Soviet Union, property belongs to the state, and orchestral musicians play instruments that are not their private property. They were astounded and envious to learn that the beautiful, priceless instruments the Boston musicians play were their own.

For orchestral musicians, playing concert after concert, throughout the countries of Europe, in various stages of jet lag with never enough time for sleep or to see each city visited can become very fatiguing. Touring is considered a mixed pleasure and requires a great effort on the part of both players and conductor just in terms of pure physical exertion.

The relationship between musicians and their conductor varies with each conductor's personality and is dependent on his view of the role and how well he succeeds. Musicians admired and loved Monteux. They adored Munch, who was gentle, protective, and personally generous to them. Leinsdorf remained aloof. He viewed his role as being to "direct, lead, and inspire." Accepting a suggestion that it might be beneficial for him to be closer to the musicians, he began by inviting them to lunch in small groups.

Always methodical, he began with the A's. Interest waned quickly.

Cellist Rostropovich, who has been guest conductor of the Boston Symphony, describes his view of being a conductor as "an older member among equals." In 1929 Harvard gave an honorary doctorate to Serge Koussevitzky, and everyone knew he liked to be addressed as Dr. Koussevitzky. In an expansive mood one day at rehearsal he suggested that he and the musicians address each other by their first names. It was no problem for the conductor, but what should they call him? "Why, Serge Alexandrovitch, of course." Somehow Dr. Koussevitzky seemed easier!

Dimitri Mitropoulos, who died in 1960, was one of the orchestra's most successful guest conductors. Conductor of the New York Philharmonic at the time, he came to Boston in 1936 and caused such a sensation that after his second visit Koussevitzky was jealous and would not invite him back. He even complained to the musicians that their playing had deteriorated terribly under the two weeks of Mitropoulos's direction. However, the players respected this great musician and they loved him too. He considered it a conductor's duty to know his players, and at the first rehearsal he greeted each man personally; on the train between New York and Boston he had memorized the name of each.

By the nature of his profession, a musician leads a partially isolated existence. He works when his neighbor does not. In a city like Boston, one of the centers of music education, players are less isolated. Sixty members of the orchestra are currently active as teachers. This is twice as many as twenty years ago. There are several chamber music groups and a jazz quartet. A number of the musicians are in demand as soloists. It is not unusual to look at a New York newspaper and see the name of first flutist Doriot Anthony Dwyer or clarinetist Harold Wright scheduled to be soloist with a chamber group there. Many individuals spend time playing in various local schools and hospitals as part of what they feel is the orchestra's obligation to its community. The community has always taken pride in its orchestra, supported it well, and offered the musicians the respect and courtesy due an honored profession. New members of the orchestra are always pleasantly surprised to find that mortgages are readily available to them, and, in the days before credit cards, a charge account at any of Boston's large stores was automatic. How many cities have a subway stop called Symphony?

In the early days, rehearsals were open to those invited by the conductor, trustees, or management. As the week's schedule progressed and the pressure of the performance became greater, so the audience increased. It obviously included those with a genuine interest in the process of making music, but it also included those whose enjoyment stemmed from the tirades of the conductor and the anguish of the players. In Koussevitzky's time a rehearsal was broadcast, live, on the radio. It was a real, working rehearsal and the conductor spared no one. Listeners at home heard several of his chilling "But my dear friends, you are very not together." One musician returned home to be greeted by his small son, who was weeping. "Daddy," he asked, "what is the matter with you, why can't you play together?" When the orchestra joined the union in 1942, the musicians quickly imposed a ban on all visitors to rehearsals. Ever since, preparation for concerts has taken place in a private and professional atmosphere.

If a musician is asked what music he enjoys playing most, the answer may well be similar to Fernand Gillet's "I like nice music, whatever it is." But variety is also very important. Not all works demand the whole orchestra. The early Haydn and Mozart symphonies, for instance, require a reduced group. During concerts there is an inevitable period of waiting around for those who are not playing but who must remain throughout the program. This time is usually spent playing cards — tense, sophisticated games of bridge interrupted only by the need to go onstage and perform.

During the Second World War the orchestra suffered none of the terrible problems it had during the First. The only incidents involving "The Star-Spangled Banner" were quite different. In 1941 Koussevitzky became an American citizen. When he raised his baton for the first work at rehearsal the following day, the musicians broke out into the national anthem. Fortunately, he recognized it and was very moved. This was in contrast to another occasion, when the musicians played "Happy Birthday" as a surprise on the appropriate day. Koussevitzky did not recognize the tune and became confused and cross. During the war, Stravinsky made a version of "The Star-Spangled Banner," which was performed by the

Boston Symphony.   There was some public protest in the press about his unorthodox version.   It turned out that there is in Massachusetts a law and a $100 fine for "rearranging" the national anthem.   At the next concert two rather surprised policemen were in the auditorium to prevent its repetition.

The performance of one piece above all others emphasized the effect of the war.   Bohuslav Martinů's Concerto for Two Pianos was due to be performed in Paris when Hitler's armies marched into Austria and prevented the publishers from sending out the music. In 1938 the performance scheduled in Prague was canceled by Hitler's invasion.   In Paris the scheduled performance coincided with that city's occupation and was not heard.   At last, in November 1941, the work received its world première in Symphony Hall, Boston.

Since the 1950s musicians, especially American ones, have been challenged by the demands of long-playing records, radio, and television.   Each time the Boston orchestra plays a concert in Symphony Hall, a tape recorder is running.   In previous years, when a musician had a bad day and fluffed a passage, only a few within the hall might have caught it and, in the overall effect of the concert, forgotten it immediately.   Not so with the advent of the tape recorder; it remembers relentlessly.   The long-playing record and the television camera represent a vast and discerning audience, not only in this country, but in music-loving communities throughout the world.   More than ever before, American orchestras today may be compared to a big, smoothly running precision instrument.   No more *grève-perlée*.   And no longer is there room in large orchestras for the eccentric performer who may play beautifully one day and be a disaster the next.   Increasingly, the success of American orchestras rests on the sustained, high-level performance of each individual musician.

Sir Thomas Beecham conducted the Boston Symphony on several occasions.   After one particularly successful program the audience would not let him go, recalling him time and again.   Finally he signaled for silence and said, "Ladies and Gentlemen, when I was a very young conductor, I heard a deaf vicar in the front row say to his neighbor, 'Why is he bowing?   The musicians did all the work.' So I shall now leave, and you may applaud these gentlemen to your hearts' content."

FIFTH SEASON

The ARTHUR FIEDLER

ESPLANADE CONCERTS

ARTHUR FIEDLER

WITH

FIFTY MEMBERS OF THE BOSTON SYMPHONY ORCHESTRA

JULY 9 to 28

NIGHTLY EXCEPT SATURDAY

8.30 — 10 P.M.

CHARLES RIVER BASIN
EMBANKMENT ROAD, FOOT OF MOUNT VERNON STREET

NO ADMISSION FEE

Poster of an early Esplanade concert with the young Arthur Fiedler conducting, about 1934.

Chapter Eight

"Evening at Symphony"

"This eternal progress and regress and progress again seems to be the most cheering thing in our lives here. I've always been saying to myself 'What next? Come, move on. This is good, but what is next?'"
— Major Higginson

LISTENING TO MUSIC as a complete activity is a sophisticated and recent occurrence in the history of man, beginning with solo and orchestral concerts. Listening means more than just hearing. Listening to music is essentially an evocative, emotional experience, one of participation and response that has its base in the memory of feelings. The eye delights in new sensation. Not so the ear, which seeks patterns and is grateful for repetition. If in hearing a new piece the ear does not recognize a familiar structure or pattern, the listener is prevented from participating and responding and so is unable to find the significance or meaning of the whole. The only way to identify a piece of music as having been written by Beethoven, Bruckner, or Stravinsky is by repeated hearing of his works. Only as the patterns and relationships become familiar does the music itself become evocative and significant. This is why most people go to concerts to hear a beautiful performance of music that they know.

Beethoven's Third Symphony, the *Eroica,* received its first performance in the spring of 1805. One of the reviewers described it this way:

> This long composition, extremely difficult of performance, is in reality a tremendously expanded, daring and wild fantasia. It lacks nothing in the way of startling and beautiful passages, in which the energetic and talented composer must be recognized; but often it loses itself in lawlessness . . . The reviewer belongs to Herr van

> Beethoven's sincerest admirers, but in this composition he must confess that he finds too much that is glaring and bizarre, which hinders greatly one's grasp of the whole, and a sense of unity is almost completely lost.

A member of the audience, who had paid one kreutzer to attend the concert, shouted out during the symphony that he would gladly give two "if the thing will but stop." Another critic reported that this was Beethoven's masterpiece,

> and if it does not please now, it is because the public is not cultured enough, artistically, to grasp all these lofty beauties; after a few thousand years have passed it will not fail in its effect . . . The public and Herr van Beethoven, who conducted, were not satisfied with each other on this evening; the public thought the symphony too heavy, too long, and himself too discourteous, because he did not nod his head in recognition of the applause which came from a portion of the audience. On the contrary, Beethoven found that the applause was not strong enough.

To the complaint that the symphony was too long, Beethoven replied, "If I write a symphony an hour long, it will be found short enough." He was not the only composer who was the target of such complaints. After the first performance of a symphony by Anton Bruckner, someone asked the composer if he didn't think it was really too long. "On the contrary," snapped Bruckner, "it is you who are too short."

The stories describing the anguish of first performances are legion. That the first performance of the *Eroica* could be thought controversial now seems amazing. The uproar over the première of Stravinsky's *Rite of Spring* seems almost quaint in light of the most recent demands and developments in the performance of orchestral music. But probably each one of us has had at least one experience at a concert where the music has seemed to disintegrate into the lawlessness of unrelated sounds due to the lack of anything familiar.

The acceptance of new music by the general public has always been much slower than its creators would like. And this lack of acceptance has not been limited to audiences. It is far more reliable and rewarding for a conductor to prepare and perform a well-loved work than to brave the new dialectics of an unproven contemporary. Composers themselves have not been noted for their sympathy for the music of others. The American composer Edward MacDowell was so averse to the music of his contemporary Brahms that he taught his dog to play dead at the sound of the German composer's name.

It did not take the predicted few thousand years for the public to become familiar enough with the lofty beauties of the *Eroica* to grasp it. The symphony soon became established as one of the monumental works of the orchestral repertory. It does not fail in its effect, but it was only with repeated listening that audiences came to recognize and understand its greatness.

The *Eroica* was played by the Boston Symphony for the first time on November 18, 1881, within the first month of its establishment. It was, with all of Beethoven's symphonies (except the Ninth), repeated each year so that Boston audiences could learn to know and appreciate its greatness.

Major Higginson founded the Boston Symphony to be "a valuable institution of art education." Its purpose was to give concerts of the highest caliber at prices within the reach of all and thereby assist in the education of a nation, which was at the time, in regard to music, singularly backward. Part of Major Higginson's plan was for the orchestra to play across the river in Cambridge for the benefit of the Harvard University community, and thus expose the young men there to what he as a young man had discovered in Europe.

From the very beginning, the orchestra sold all the tickets to its concert series at the Music Hall. With its stated policy of reaching as many people as possible, the outward thrust began immediately.

Initially, concerts were given in towns near Boston; later they extended north, south, and west to areas where concert music had never been played, where, to encourage an audience, the musicians were expected to parade like minstrels. These tours were further expanded as the orchestra became more famous. In 1893 the Boston Symphony was invited to play in Chicago at the World's Fair, and in 1915 it crossed the continent in a special train to play a series of concerts in San Francisco under Karl Muck. The way in which it has reached out to new audiences is a vital part of the orchestra's story and success. In the early days, the only way to increase the audience was to travel and add to the number of subscription series at the Music Hall. In the 1880s one of the popular ways to reach new audiences was by giving benefits to raise money for specific projects. In 1886 there was a benefit to aid the victims of a recent flood in Roxbury. Another was held to raise money to erect a monument to Mozart in Vienna. There were also festivals that featured music by one composer. The Boston Pops, a relaxed series of more popular compositions, began in 1885 as a way to provide employment for the musicians during the summer months and also to serve as a training ground for new listeners. Audiences were allowed to eat and drink during the programs. The Pops was not held in the summer of 1890 because a license for wine was not forthcoming from the authorities. The concerts did take place from 1919 to 1933 ("the dry years") and a most unctuous contemporary description of the Pops went as follows: "During Prohibition the Pops has had an increased and more musically discerning patronage."

Only when Arthur Fiedler took over the Pops concerts in 1930 did they begin to enjoy the extraordinary success that has continued ever since. Youth concerts began in 1886, when one Saturday afternoon in May 2500 grade school children came to the Music Hall. The series was not maintained at the time but was reinstated briefly by Monteux and then again in 1959 by Harry Ellis Dickson, assistant conductor of the Pops and violinist in the Boston Symphony. It continues under Dickson's direction, and he conducts and provides the commentary for the series. It began with six concerts a season and has now expanded to fifteen, reaching 39,000 local children a season.

The notion of enjoying a live concert at home goes way back to 1884, when the telephone was just coming into use. Someone designed a scheme for making a telephone connection between the Music Hall and the private residences of those who might like to listen at home. The scheme was not accomplished because at that time it was not yet known how to amplify transmitted sound. But technology advanced quickly to make the concerts of the Boston Symphony available on a more general basis. At the turn of the century the fame of the orchestra was spreading, if a little erratically. In 1909 a small town near Boston wrote to the management of the orchestra, announcing that it was going to have a concert and a dance and that the people of the town had heard that the Boston Symphony was a good orchestra; they were willing to pay $300 if the orchestra would play both the concert and for the dancing after. It turned out that the orchestra did have a prior engagement that night, to play in New York's Carnegie Hall.

Much has been written about the Boston Symphony audiences, in particular the Friday afternoon audience. It is a very polite audience and can always find something to applaud, even if it is only the fact that the music is over. Just before the last movement of the final work, even of Beethoven's Ninth, many of the ladies, who comprise a great part of the matinée audience, leave "to get ahead of the rush." And moving the start of the concert from two-thirty to two o'clock has had no effect on the exodus. A critic once suggested that there be a concert of just final movements so that the ladies could at last hear them. The concert would then end with a first movement; thus the ladies would not miss anything they had

The ladies of the Friday afternoon audience.

The Esplanade shell in the 1950s.

not already heard. Cleveland Amory, in *The Proper Bostonians*, further describes the typical lady:

> For more than half a century, attired in her sensible coat, her sensible hat and her sensible shoes, she has entered the hall promptly at 2:25 and swept serenely to her seat in a manner that defies description. If she forgets her ticket it is no tragedy. A large proportion of patrons regularly do this, but they have been so resolutely marching toward the same seats for so many years that no usher, even in a packed hall, would dare attempt to stop them.

The ladies smile at their own description. As only a part of the vast total audience they are a loyal segment that channels its sensible energies into the various fund-raising activities that help support the orchestra. In 1889 Major Higginson described the audience another way:

> Several times when I have faltered in my plan for the future, I have taken heart again on seeing the crowd of young, fresh school girls, of music students, of tired school teachers, of weary men, of little old ladies leading grey lives not often reached by the sunshine, and I have said to myself, "One year more anyway."

And another time he responded to a musician who had urged him to admit to the concerts only the truly poor: "If a series of concerts were offered at low prices only to the truly poor, do you suppose that anyone but the truly rich would frequent them?"

In the first years of the orchestra there were approximately 5000 subscribers. Now there are 215,000 subscribers to concerts held in Symphony Hall. Close to 135,000 additional people hear the orchestra on its regular trips to New York and Providence.

Initially the orchestra gave twenty concerts. Now its members play roughly two hundred and twenty concerts a year. The increase in numbers of performances occurred slowly over the years, as the demand for concerts became apparent. The Boston Symphony was the first to have a fifty-two week season, and it plays in a variety of locations. During the winter months there are eight different subscription series in Symphony Hall. These include eight Open Rehearsals on Wednesday evenings, which benefit the orchestra's Pension Fund. In the spring the musicians (except for the first-chair players) discard their black coats for blue ones and play fifty-four concerts as the Boston Pops, conducted by Arthur Fiedler. For two weeks in July there are free Esplanade concerts at the foot of Beacon Hill, at the Hatch Memorial Shell on the Charles

Aerial view of the July 4, 1976, Independence Day concert on the Esplanade (*Ted Dully*).

River Embankment. Arthur Fiedler started these concerts in 1929, the year before he became director of the Pops. From July through Labor Day, the orchestra moves to its summer home, Tanglewood, in Lenox, Massachusetts. The orchestra first participated in the Berkshire Festival in 1936, and except for the years during World War II, it has given its series of twenty-four concerts every Friday and Saturday evening and Sunday afternoon. Running concurrently with the Berkshire Festival is the Berkshire Music Center, an intensive training program for musicians given by an impressive faculty of conductors, composers, and performers, many from the orchestra. Hundreds of distinguished musicians throughout the world have studied there.

Back in Boston in the fall, the Boston Symphony Chamber Players — the orchestra's solo timpanist and the principal string, woodwind, and brass players — give their series of programs. And the Young People's concerts begin once more to train young audiences.

Nearly two hundred and fifty performances a year is very close to the limit that can be scheduled and also allow for adequate rest and rehearsal for the musicians. One should remember that they use their bodies when they play. A fine brass or woodwind player can't play to the last five percent of capacity so frequently and not experience great fatigue.

In 1805, Beethoven's *Eroica* took approximately fifty-five minutes to be performed. Today, more than one hundred and seventy years later, it still requires the same number of musicians and the same amount of time. Making music is different from making toothpaste. Music is not governed by industry's rule of thumb: more is better and quicker is more. A symphony orchestra is what is called a labor-intensive industry, which means that adding musicians to the orchestra does not make either better or more music, nor does playing the music faster make "more" music. There also comes a time when it is not possible to schedule any more concerts into a week or a year.

Reasonably priced tickets do not bring in enough money to cover the cost of giving concerts — and those costs continue to rise. Major Higginson understood this, and as its benefactor he paid that portion of the bills not covered by the orchestra's income. His commitment to the concept of having a great orchestra in Boston was such that he could exclaim, "Never mind the balance sheet!

A Pops prank with Arthur Fiedler in the 1970s *(Michael Pierce).*

Charge the deficit, if there be any, to profit and forget the loss, for it does not really exist." And for him it did not.

After Major Higginson's death, the nine trustees carried on his policies and followed his directions as best they could, recalling his words. "Find a great artist who is eager to devote his very life to the Orchestra's perfection. Give him absolute freedom in his quest, subject only to the limits of the available budget."

In 1934 the Boston philanthropist Ernest B. Dane gave the orchestra a substantial gift, $100,000, which finally made the Boston Symphony sole owners of Symphony Hall. That same year the orchestra reached out to its loyal audiences and asked them to become members of the Friends of the Boston Symphony by contributing to its support. That first year 647 people became Friends. By 1949 there were 3300. In 1976 more than 8000 people, through various fund-raising events, contributed $1,690,247 to the orchestra.

The management of an orchestra has always been a complicated process. In nineteenth-century Europe, managers of opera houses were said to be assured of only two things: it would be exciting and eventually the theater would burn down. The oil lamps in wooden buildings made this almost inevitable. In 1830 the man who was invited to take over the management of the Italian Opera Company in London for three years responded to his potential employers, "Give me such terms as will secure a provision for my family, and three months to make a tour of all the mad houses and select one

Students on the grounds of Tanglewood, near the main administrative building.

which I should prefer for my final retreat; and then I may talk with you."

The administration of the Boston Symphony is not that terrifying. Koussevitzky once told a trustee, "My dear sir, music is a 'paraseet' that take many monies." It also requires a support system that involves a great deal more than one might think pertains to the performance of music. For instance, the orchestra's business includes the management of real estate. The Boston Symphony owns, in addition to Symphony Hall, the giant Music Shed, theater, chamber music hall, and the complex of education buildings at Tanglewood. It may be the only orchestra to own a seven-gang lawn mower to mow the forty acres of lawn surrounding those buildings. As well as the long-range and day-to-day functions of the orchestra, the management is very much involved in the distribution of the orchestra's music in this country and abroad. In the early days that meant the tours to other cities, the intent of which

Gunther Schuller, former director of the New England Conservatory of Music, Seiji Ozawa, and Leonard Bernstein at Tanglewood.

was primarily educational. To a great degree the recording industry has taken over that educational function. Because of its records, the orchestra's performances are known by music lovers around the world. The motive now for touring is that of any star performer — to be seen, to show off. And with jet planes it is almost as easy to play in Vienna as it is in Detroit.

The recording industry has had a tremendous and continuing impact on the lives of music lovers and orchestras. The invention of the phonograph by Edison occurred in 1877, four years before the first concert by the Boston Symphony. In 1891 selections from the *Eroica* were recorded on Edison cylinders in Carnegie Hall. In 1900 the flat disc was invented. In 1914 Arthur Nikisch in Berlin recorded Beethoven's Fifth Symphony. By 1925, recording had switched from being acoustical to electrical, and the large orchestras in this country had all made recordings by the middle twenties. In September 1917, Karl Muck and the Boston Symphony went to Camden, New Jersey, to make their first recording with the Victor Talking Machine Company. It was a very hot day, and the men had to be crowded into the acoustical shell, which looked like half a ball open at one end. The first-desk men sat outside the ball on high stools, playing directly into horns of their own. The others, when they had solos, had to run out, blow into the horn, and run quietly back. The orchestra played Tchaikovsky's Fourth Symphony, a curious choice since Muck did not like the work. He was in formal dress and was so fascinated by the turntable making the master disc that he kept turning to watch it. When the musicians listened to the playback later, they were amazed by what they heard.

Since that first session, the orchestra has sold more than fifty million recordings. Until 1935 the orchestra always traveled to Camden to record. But in February 1935, RCA Victor brought its recording equipment to Symphony Hall, thus taking advantage of the extraordinary acoustics, and since then the recordings have been made there. One of the works recorded at the first session in Symphony Hall was Richard Strauss's *Also Sprach Zarathustra*, on nine twelve-inch 78 rpm records! Each season the orchestra, which now records for Deutsche Grammophon, makes between five and ten records.

The long-playing record, high fidelity equipment, television, and radio have continued and made possible on a national and international level what Major Higginson set out to do for his fellow citizens of Boston, to make good music available at reasonable prices. The first radio broadcasts of the orchestra came in 1926, when, with a private gift of $12,000, the Saturday evening concerts were broadcast live. In 1958 the orchestra set up the Boston Symphony Transcription Trust, which makes tapes of the orchestra's concerts available to radio stations anywhere in the world. The proceeds of the trust benefit the Pension Fund. The orchestra's concerts are broadcast live by WGBH in Boston, and with WCRB, also of Boston, they are broadcast in multiplex stereo, providing four different channels of sound.

The Boston Symphony was the pioneer in the making and distribution of its televised concerts. In 1962 and 1963 twenty-six programs were made for syndication; they were seen in more than forty cities in the United States and Canada as well as in twenty

Aerial view of Tanglewood, summer home of the orchestra.

Jordan Whitelaw, producer of *Evening at Symphony*, with the WGBH-FM mobile unit at Tanglewood.

other countries. In 1967, the NBC special from Tanglewood won a Peabody Award. In 1976 Seiji Ozawa won an Emmy for "outstanding achievement in music direction" with Charles Ives's *Central Park in the Dark* and Richard Strauss's *Ein Heldenleben*. This program was part of the series *Evening at Symphony*, produced by WGBH, Boston, and the Boston Symphony Orchestra with Seiji Ozawa, music director. This was the first regularly scheduled television series devoted exclusively to the performance of classical music. Usually the program is an hour long, but during the season there are several ninety-minute specials, which have included complete performances of Beethoven's Ninth Symphony, Brahms's *German Requiem,* and Berlioz's *Romeo and Juliet.* In each thirteen-week segment Seiji Ozawa conducts at least seven of the programs. Other conductors have included former music directors William Steinberg and Erich Leinsdorf; the orchestra's principal guest conductor, Colin Davis; and Michael Tilson Thomas and Claudio Abbado. Some of the piano soloists who have appeared on the program are Vladimir Ashkenazy, Peter Serkin, Misha Dichter, and Alexis Weissenberg; concertmaster Joseph Silverstein has been the soloist in Elgar's Violin Concerto in B Minor and the Schönberg Violin Concerto. The music ranges from the best-known, well-loved works of Beethoven, Berlioz, and Brahms to the less familiar music of Tippett, Crumb, and Takemitsu.

Evening at Symphony is a product of WGBH, Boston, and the orchestral camera treatment is by Jordan M. Whitelaw, producer. Whitelaw, now a free-lance television producer, was on the staff of WGBH-FM when it went on the air in 1951. Two years later he took over the production of the Boston Symphony radio broadcasts and in 1953 he moved over to the staff of the Boston Symphony. He pioneered their television programs. He describes himself as having an exceptionally good ear for "canned" music, and as a child he knew that Toscanini's broadcasts from the much-touted Studio 8H "shouldn't have happened to a dog; the studio was acoustically dead — dry." Whitelaw started to go to the orchestra's concerts as a junior in high school. Now he enjoys working with the orchestra and with the warm sound of the large hall. It is he who sets and has maintained the superlative standards of the orchestra's broadcasts and telecasts, a standard that has not been attained elsewhere. A stately man, and an outspoken one with a booming voice, Whitelaw knows exactly what he wants in a telecast and how to achieve it. It is he who writes the scripts for the telecasts and decides on all the camera shots and the close-up effects. His aim is for the visual images to follow the movement of the music so that the viewer will know more about the music than before. A multiplicity of camera shots is confusing. It is important not to show too much too quickly, which would detract from the sound of the music. One of the aspects of performance that attracts visual attention is the spectacle of an entire section playing together. All the French horns or all the violins, performing at once, is a graceful sight. The percussion is fun to watch, and the conductor is always a point of focus. He is interesting to watch in any particularly rhythmical section or in times of transition, and of course at any dramatic moments in the music.

Setting up cameras onstage for the filming of *Evening at Symphony*.

To watch the preparation for a telecast is completely absorbing. In the winter of 1977, Klaus Tennstedt was filmed conducting Mahler's Fourth Symphony. Several weeks prior to the telecast Whitelaw made his preparations. Since there is no recording of Tennstedt conducting Mahler's Fourth, he used a tape of another performance. For many hours he listened to the music while following the score in order to decide which instrument might be featured appropriately for a particular visual effect. Mahler's music is usually very dense and so complex that it is impossible to show everything. On the other hand, to follow the motifs in Mahler's music is interesting to see as well as to hear. By the time the orchestra rehearses the work with Tennstedt, the camera plan has been made. During the orchestral rehearsals, Whitelaw follows his score to see and hear any variation in tempo or emphasis that the conductor makes in his interpretation of the work, as opposed to the interpretation on the tape used for preparation. Another aspect of the performance that Whitelaw watches closely in rehearsal is the points in the score at which the conductor becomes particularly moved or excited by the music, which he may wish to include on a close-up. Thursday night's concert is audiotaped, and on Saturday, the day of the telecast of the live performance, the production crew meets at noon in Symphony Hall to get its instructions and go through sequences of shots to catch any particularly difficult transitions.

The television presentation of the Mahler Fourth includes two hundred and twenty-seven different camera shots and effects. Five cameras are set up in Symphony Hall: one on each side of the front of the first balcony; a camera backstage, which is focused on the conductor and is recorded on videotape separately in case another camera loses the picture. Another camera on the side is halfway back in the auditorium and is used mostly for the concertmaster, the first violins, and the basses. Camera two is high above the second balcony at the back of the hall in a recessed alcove reached only by a narrow iron walkway. Two of the cameramen have been with the production unit since the program's inception ten years ago, the others almost as long. They know the orchestra members by face as well as name and they know the difference between a clarinet and an oboe, so any last-minute seating change a conductor may make does not necessarily cause a problem. One of the extraordinary facts about *Evening at Symphony* is that there is no camera rehearsal with the musicians. This is something that film professionals who watch the program find hard to believe. At 3:00 P.M. on Saturday there is a camera runthrough. Using the audiotape of Thursday night for the sound, the crew goes through all two hundred and twenty-seven successive camera shots, focusing on empty chairs that have a Magic Marker sign that may read: CELLO I, TRUMPET II, BASS, or whatever. To give the cameramen some human scale, the stage manager sits on a high stool on the podium, quietly reading science fiction. Outside Symphony Hall the production crew is in Channel 2's mobile unit, a traveling studio that contains the necessary broadcast equipment. Across one end of the mobile unit are the television monitors, seven in all. One shows the shot that is being prepared to go on the air, one shows what is actually being telecast, and the others see what each of the other cameras sees. In front of the monitors sits the crew, all members wearing headsets to hear and microphones to speak to the cameramen.

The assistant director's job is to reaffirm the written directions each cameraman has, cuing them before each shot — for example, "Camera one on oboes with effects." Beside him sits the score reader, who moves his pencil with the progress of the music, letting the director know exactly where they are in relation to the scheduled shots, which are written into the score. The director has studied the score and knows the sequence of shots and the music involved. It is he who coordinates the proceedings, snapping his fingers to indicate the end of a shot and counting the time during an eventual close-up, and he instructs the cameramen about how to frame the various effects in their cameras. Beside the director sits Kathy Smith, the "switcher," a big woman with delicate hands and a quick mind who runs the controls that switch from one shot to the next, dividing the screen to include the pictures from two different cameras, and making the final technical adjustments, controlling what goes out on the air. She watches all the monitors at once with particular concern for the cue monitor, constantly adjusting controls. There is one particular effects shot in the Mahler that takes some minutes to work out. During the third movement there is a trio with oboe, English horn, and French horn that is very beautiful, and Whitelaw has decided that each of the instruments should be seen on the screen. The problem is that the players don't sit next to each other, so it will take the pictures of three cameras to produce the effect, with the English horn player framed in a diamond between the other two. Finally, with production assistants sitting in for the musicians, the possibility of the effect is achieved and the rehearsal ends. Everyone breaks for dinner before the concert.

Backstage before the concert musicians arrive and begin to tune up. Klaus Tennstedt walks to the door on the edge of the stage to look at the very bright television lights. Jordan Whitelaw talks to some of the musicians. It is clear that they have enormous respect for the sustained high quality of his work. The players trust his knowledge and his taste in the visual portrayal of the orchestra, which is intelligent and sensitive. Once the musicians wanted to make him a formal member of the orchestra, an honor he would have enjoyed. Whitelaw has worked with many conductors and found some easier than others. Both Leinsdorf and Steinberg were extremely well organized and respected the difficulties of telecasting.   In the early days of telecasting Charles Munch was the music director and he assumed that the camera and Whitelaw could manage anything.   Once, during a telecast of Beethoven's Seventh Symphony, he cut the scherzo and told no one but the musicians. When it came time for the scherzo, the cameramen and crew were thrown suddenly into confusion.   Munch didn't really care about television, and when he didn't care he didn't understand English. There are times currently when Ozawa has trouble deciding on the placement of choruses or the orchestra's seating plan, and these last-minute decisions make for tense moments before a program.

Jordan Whitelaw supervises an early television taping.

Fortunately, the telecasts have been remarkably free from even trivial errors. But there have been occasional slips. Once, during Brahms's D Minor Piano Concerto, the French horns switched their parts without telling anyone and the camera zoomed in for a close-up for the solo on the first horn, not realizing that the third horn was going to play it. There on camera was the first horn shaking the saliva out of the bell of his instrument while his colleague played the solo off camera. In some music such as the Elgar Second Symphony it is very difficult to separate individual sounds. The music is so dense that the sound is almost opaque. Haydn and Mozart are much easier to film than more complicated, later works, but there are times, in minuets, for instance, when a phrase may be repeated several times; the ear likes it but the eye needs variety.

As the moment of the performance approaches, Whitelaw returns to the mobile unit, admonishing the timpanist Arthur Press in his booming voice, "Okay, Arthur, now when you play the triangle don't hold it down by your knees — please hold it up; I have to see it." In the mobile unit the production crew has gathered and is talking animatedly to the engineers and the cameramen. There is a sense of tension, excitement, and anticipation as the concert is about to begin. But there is also a calmness to the proceedings that comes from the professional pride and past success of the participants. The concert begins as Klaus Tennstedt walks to the podium, bows to the audience, and raises his arms. The sleigh bells jingle and the Mahler has begun. In the mobile unit the quiet voices of the production crew giving instructions and cues, the switcher's hands dextrously fading, dissolving, cutting, and sharpening the effects, all have an internal rhythm as smooth as the flow of the music itself. The time spent at the camera runthrough was well spent and the aural effect of the music is now enhanced by the sensitive choice of camera shots. Whitelaw sits behind the crew, listening and watching it all unfold. If there should be an equipment failure, it will be he who steps in and improvises the shots to cover for the ailing equipment. The music continues. The assistant director cues "139 on 1, effects on Press." Camera one focuses on Arthur Press, who is holding the triangle below his waist. As he strikes it he lifts it high and the crew smiles. Tension mounts as the complicated trio draws close. The switcher frames the delicately balanced picture from the three cameras, placing the English horn player deftly in the center of the diamond. It switches from the cue monitor to the transmission monitor and there is a low cheer. It is perfect. The Mahler moves on toward its gentle ending. At the close of the concert the audience rises to applaud a most moving performance. Inside the mobile unit there is exhilaration at having done a difficult job superbly. Everyone thanks everyone for his or her part of the production. One by one the monitor screens go dark and the control board is turned off. Happily, the crew steps into the night and heads home.

The Boston Symphony Orchestra began its life almost one hundred years ago — the dream of one brave man who wished to serve his fellow citizens. Now, for twenty-six weeks each season, the Boston Symphony reaches millions of music lovers in this country and Canada who each week look forward to their *Evening at Symphony*. Major Higginson's dream has become one of the great public service institutions of America and has been designated a National Treasure by its government. What was the gift of one has been accepted by all. And in the partnership of public and private support it continues to serve "In the Interest of Good Music."

Major Higginson was a private man, seldom sharing his feelings publicly, seldom writing his feelings for music. But he did once write to a friend about his favorite symphony:

> As to the "Eroica," I had meant to tell you how I felt about it, but it opens the flood-gates, and I can't. The wail of grief, and then the sympathy which should comfort the sufferer. The wonderful funeral dirge, so solemn, so full, so deep, so splendid, and always with courage and comfort. The delightful march home from the grave in the scherzo — the wild Hungarian, almost gypsy in tone — and then the climax of the melody, where the gates of Heaven open, and we see the angels singing and reaching their hands to us with perfect welcome. No words are of any avail, and never does that passage of entire relief and joy come to me without tears — and I wait for it through life, and hear it, and wonder —

Bibliography
Index

Bibliography

Bekker, Paul. *The Story of the Orchestra.* W. W. Norton, 1936.

Cairns, David, editor and translator. *Memoirs of Hector Berlioz.* Knopf, 1969.

Carse, Adam. *The Orchestra in the XVIII Century.* W. Heffer, 1940.

——— . *The Orchestra, From Beethoven to Berlioz.* W. Heffer, 1948.

David, Hans T., and Arthur Mendel, editors. *The Bach Reader.* W.W. Norton, 1966.

Dickson, Harry Ellis. *Gentlemen More Dolce Please!* Beacon Press, 1969.

Forbes, Elliot. *Thayer's Life of Beethoven.* Princeton, 1967.

Gehringer, Karl. *Haydn: A Creative Life in Music.* W. W. Norton, 1946.

Grout, Donald. *A History of Western Music.* W. W. Norton, 1964.

Hart, Philip. *Orpheus in the New World.* W. W. Norton, 1973.

Higginson, Mary. *Thomas Wentworth Higginson.* Houghton Mifflin, 1914.

Higginson, Thomas. *Cheerful Yesterdays.* Houghton Mifflin, 1898.

Howe, M. A. deWolf. *The Boston Symphony Orchestra.* Houghton Mifflin, 1931.

Johnson, H. Earle. *Symphony Hall, Boston.* Little, Brown, 1950.

——— . *Musical Interludes in Boston 1795–1830.* Columbia University Press, 1943.

Leinsdorf, Erich. *Cadenza.* Houghton Mifflin, 1976.

Morgenstern, Sam, editor. *Composers on Music.* Pantheon, 1956.

Munch, Charles. *I Am a Conductor.* Oxford University Press, 1955.

Perry, Bliss. *Life and Letters of Henry Lee Higginson.* Atlantic Monthly Press, 1921.

Schonberg, Harold. *The Great Conductors.* Simon & Schuster, 1967.

Smith, Moses. *Koussevitzky.* Allen Towne & Heath, 1947.

Grove's Dictionary of Music & Musicians. Presser, 1916.

Grove's Dictionary of Music & Musicians. St. Martin's Press, 1959.

Harvard Graduates Magazine. Vol. 28, March 1920.

Index

W